CROSS☩ROADS

Church History

Author
Richard J. Reichert

BROWN-ROA
A Division of Harcourt Brace & Company

Our Mission

The primary mission of BROWN-ROA is to provide the Catholic and Christian educational markets with the highest quality catechetical print and media resources. The content of these resources reflects the best insights of current theology, methodology, and pedagogical research. The resources are practical and easy to use, designed to meet expressed market needs, and written to reflect the teachings of the Catholic Church.

Nihil Obstat
Rev. Richard L. Schaefer

Imprimatur
✠ Most Rev. Jerome Hanus, O.S.B.
Archbishop of Dubuque
January 4, 1998
Feast of Saint Elizabeth Ann Seton

The Imprimatur is an official declaration that a book or pamphlet is free of doctrinal or moral error. No implication is contained therein that anyone who granted the Imprimatur agrees with the contents, opinions, or statements expressed.

Copyright © 1999 by BROWN-ROA, a division of Harcourt Brace & Company

All rights reserved. No part of this publication may be reproduced or transmitted in any form or by any means, electronic or mechanical, including photocopy, recording, or any information storage and retrieval system, without permission in writing from the publisher.

Requests for permission to make copies of any part of the work should be mailed to the following address: Permissions Department, Harcourt Brace & Company, 6277 Sea Harbor Drive, Orlando, Florida 32887-6777.

Portions of this work were published in previous editions.

Excerpts from the English translation of the *Catechism of the Catholic Church* for use in the United States of America Copyright © 1994, United States Catholic Conference, Inc.—Libreria Editrice Vaticana. Used with Permission.

The Scripture quotations contained herein are from the New Revised Standard Version Bible: Catholic Edition copyright © 1993 and 1989 by the Division of Christian Education of the National Council of the Churches of Christ in the U.S.A. Used by permission. All rights reserved.

Illustrations: Rob Suggs

Photo Credits: Maryknoll—26; Gene Plaisted, OSC/CROSIERS—16, 20, 28, 31, 31, 39, 99; James L. Shaffer—2, 4, 14, 21, 33, 36, 41, 46, 55, 66, 75, 83, 85, 96, 100

Printed in the United States of America

ISBN 0-15-950472-4

10 9 8 7 6 5 4 3

WHAT'S TO COME IN HISTORY

Introduction: Once upon a Time iv
- You are invited to a special celebration
- Tell me a story

1: A Patchwork Quilt—A Common Thread 1
- How do important events form a life quilt?
- What is the thread that joins our community?

2: The First Hundred Years—33–100 C.E. 10
- When do we celebrate the birthday of the Church?
- How did the first disciples spread the gospel message in the Roman Empire?
- What did the Council of Jerusalem establish?

3: The Courage to be Christian—100–312 C.E. 23
- What were some of the changes the community experienced?
- Who was responsible for keeping the faith alive?
- How did the persecutions help spread Christianity?

4: From Freedom to Feudalism—313–800 C.E. 36
- How did freedom of religion affect Christian life?
- What influence did the monastic movement have on the people?
- Who traveled the world to spread the message of Jesus and where did they go?

5: The Middle Ages: The Wheat and the Weeds—800–1400 C.E. ... 51
- Who ruled the Holy Roman Empire?
- How did the Church try to promote peace during a period of conflict?
- What reforms and reorganizations occurred in the Church?

6: Rebirth, Rebellion, and Reform—1400–1700 C.E. 65
- What influence did the Renaissance have on the Church?
- How did the Protestant Church begin?
- In what way did Church leaders respond to the spread of Protestantism?

7: Sacred, Secular, Scientific—1700–1950 C.E. 79
- When the Church established in the United States, how did parishes form?
- How did the reforms of the Council of Trent affect the Church?
- What were some of the challenges the Church faced?

8: Up to the Minute—1950 C.E.–Present 93
- Why did Pope John XXIII call the Second Vatican Council?
- How does the Second Vatican Council affect us today?
- What is the role of the laity in the Church today?

Appendix I: Saints for Our Time 106

Appendix II: Your Catholic Heritage 108

INTRODUCTION
Once upon a Time

YOU ARE INVITED TO A SPECIAL CELEBRATION

In honor of: You and all other young persons learning about their faith.

Theme: A historical setting sets the stage for learning the story of your ancestors and how they were able to keep the faith alive through centuries of good and bad times.

For what reason: Because your story as a Christian is part of our Church story—your life is a part of history!

What to bring: An interest in learning and a willingness to share your views.

Your host: Dick Reichert

See you there!

Tell me a story

Our lives are filled with stories. Take a moment to think back on the fairy tales you learned as a child.

What would happen if . . .
- Goldilocks ran into the Big Bad Wolf when running from the Bears' house?
- The Three Little Pigs moved in with the Three Bears?
- Little Red Riding Hood met up with Little Boy Blue?
- Little Jack Horner asked Little Miss Muffet for some curds and whey?
- Jack and Jill were sitting on the wall next to Humpty Dumpty?

In a small group, choose one of these situations (or create your own) and rewrite the story. Be prepared to share your story with the class.

Now what would happen if . . .
- Jesus came to your class to talk about how people are treated at your school?
- You were asked to be the personal assistant of the pope?
- You were the only disciple left on earth to spread the gospel message?

Share your views on these situations with the class.

Knowing that the history of the Church is our story, we begin. Once upon a time . . .

1
A PATCHWORK QUILT— A COMMON THREAD

My own "life quilt"

All of us have experienced memorable and remarkable events during our lifetime. To begin a course on the history of our Church, it is valuable to think back upon your own life and discover how past events fit together to create a personal, unique "life quilt" about you!

For each patch in the following quilt, write down memories and dates associated with each event or person in your life.

Date and place of your birth	First Eucharist	Best friend
Favorite toy	Favorite home	First day of school
Most important lesson learned	Family vacation	Junior high memory
Favorite teacher	Important people	Memorable birthday

What other patches would you add to your quilt? Why?
_____
_____

Why is learning history important?

The story of your life is much like the history of our Catholic Church. Both have been built upon past events in order to become what they are today. Learning about "what has been" in our Church will indeed help you to understand "what is" today. Additionally, studying the story of Catholicism will allow you to grow in your own knowledge and faith.

Our history as a Church has been woven together throughout the past two thousand years, influencing who we are today and what we believe in as Catholics. This course will allow you to examine our roots, meet key people, and learn about important adventures of our ancestors in faith. Learning about our history helps us understand and explain current events. Also, if we don't learn from the past, we are likely to repeat its errors and prevent ourselves from growing in new directions. As the youth of our Church, you are called to lead us into our future, equipped with knowledge and faith. This course will aid you in meeting this challenge!

TRIVIA TEASER

The dictionary defines *history* as a "chronological record of events." The oldest record discovered tells of the history of China. It is estimated to have been written before the year 1000 B.C.E.

Dialogue Corner

"If we don't learn from the past, we are likely to repeat its errors . . ."

With a partner, think of an event in history, such as the Holocaust or the AIDS situation, that we need to learn from in order to keep from repeating its effects. Discuss what we as a community can do to prevent an event like this from happening again.

What events have influenced your life and helped shape the person you are today?

Who are the key people that have influenced you? What role did they play?

What's in store for you?

This brief history of our Church invites you to:
- Discover that you are not alone in trying to keep the faith. You will gain knowledge of key people in our Church and the struggles and joys they experienced trying to keep the faith in their own lifetimes.
- Understand why the Church is the way it is. You will learn many of our traditions and past problems that have affected and continue to affect us as Catholics today.
- Perceive the work of the Holy Spirit through the centuries of the Church.
- Come to know why history is so important. You will find that history is not just "a thing of the past" but that it has much to teach us even today.

Our community quilt

The story of our Church is the story of a community of people who share one special thing in common—faith and friendship with Jesus. What this community of disciples did through the centuries, how society treated them, and the kinds of people the community considered its heroes and heroines can be traced back to that common bond—faith and friendship with Jesus. That's the common thread of our story.

In each century, this faith and friendship with Jesus is expressed in somewhat different ways. In our story, the community of disciples faced new challenges and problems every day. Instrumental in these new challenges the community faced was the leadership in society. As new leaders came to power, new laws and philosophies governed the people. These challenges did lead to some low points in our history, times when it looked as if the Church would break apart and disappear altogether. Despite these obstacles and setbacks, our story has its high points, periods in history when the community almost seemed to reach the perfection to which Jesus calls us.

As in any good story, there are villains as well as saints. Enemies inside and outside the community kept trying to break it apart and destroy it. It was the grace of the Spirit and the unity of the believers within the community that strengthened the group as a whole. It is a story full of contradiction. Saints and sinners live side by side in the community. There are acts of great love and there are acts of great cruelty.

It was almost two thousand years ago when Jesus first gathered a small community of Jews around him in Galilee. That little community has grown today to include men, women, and children from every race and every country in the world. Yet the faith and the friendship of today's disciples are essentially the same faith and friendship experienced by the little group in Galilee. They have been handed down through the centuries and kept alive from generation to generation. Language and customs change, as well as the shape of society, but Jesus remains the same—yesterday, today, and forever. True discipleship remains the same also—yesterday, today, and forever.

The story of this community truly resembles a patchwork quilt. Joined together with the common thread—God's grace and our faith and friendship with Jesus—the events and the people of the community survived and strengthened to provide us with our story, a story of discipleship, which is in keeping with God the Father's plan.

 As a disciple of Jesus, this is how I express my faith and friendship with Jesus every day:
_____
_____

TRIVIA TEASER

To translate a century to a calendar year, subtract one hundred years from the century. For example, the eighteenth century refers to the 1700s. The years 1–100 C.E. comprise the first century.

How do you study a patchwork quilt?

If we are going to trace the patchwork story of this community of disciples through a two thousand-year period, we need to approach it in an orderly manner. So in each chapter, we will look at our ancestors and their stories from five different angles.

Dialogue Corner

It is the year 2200 C.E. For vacation, you purchase tickets from TWA, Travel Worlds Away, a time machine travel agency. You and your family are going to visit your ancestors in the year 1995. From there, you plan on traveling to first-century Galilee.

- As a disciple of Jesus from the twenty-third century, how would you "fit in" with the faith community of 1995? Of first-century Galilee? Explain.

- Suppose that one of the disciples from Galilee traveled back with you. Would he or she feel at home in the faith community of 2200? Why?

- What has remained the same in our faith communities? What has changed over the years?

THE COMMUNITY'S INTERACTION WITH SOCIETY AND GOVERNMENT

At times, the Church has played a major role in shaping society. At other times, the reverse has been true—society has influenced the development of the Church. It is important that we examine the roles society and the Church play in our community and how they influence each other.

THE COMMUNITY'S SPIRITUAL LIFE

In each age, the community adapted its response to Jesus and the gospel according to its own situation. We can learn a lot by examining how our ancestors remained faithful in the situations they experienced.

THE COMMUNITY'S UNDERSTANDING OF THE GOSPEL MESSAGE

The basic message of the gospel never changes, but as times change, we find new ways to express the message so that it makes sense to the people.

THE COMMUNITY'S MISSION

Jesus gave his disciples a command that remains the same in every age: "Go therefore and make disciples of all nations, baptizing them in the name of the Father and of the Son and of the Holy Spirit, and teaching them to obey everything that I have commanded you" (Matthew 28:19–20). We will see how the community has responded to this call through the centuries.

Catechism Connection

The transmission of the Christian faith consists primarily in proclaiming Jesus Christ in order to lead others to faith in him. . . . And [the first disciples] invite people of every era to enter into the joy of their communion with Christ. (425)

THE COMMUNITY'S ORGANIZATION

Every community needs a specific way to govern itself, choose its leaders, and protect itself by establishing rules and guidelines. It is interesting to note how our Church community, with the guidance of the Holy Spirit, has accomplished this as times have changed throughout the past two thousand years.

These five aspects of community are woven together throughout history. The story of our Church is a combination of our interactions with society, the spiritual life, an understanding of the gospel message, our mission, and organization. Every aspect affects the others. So you can see why you need to look at the community of disciples from all these different angles if you want to understand it at any given time. You can also see how what happens to the community at one point plays a big role in how the community reacts in the next period. Even today we are affected by the actions and decisions of those who came before us.

What is your task?

By learning how our ancestors lived out their discipleship, we will gain some valuable help in figuring out what we must do today. If they overcame obstacles, so can we. If they made mistakes, we can learn from them. If we look at the successes and joys of their lives, we can work to achieve the same for ourselves. Your task is to learn the stories of our ancestors and to learn the valuable lessons these stories teach.

What is the common thread?

What connects you with all of your ancestors of faith is your friendship with Jesus. For two thousand years this aspect of the Church has not changed. As a member of the Church, you are a part of our community's continuing story and history. The quilt of your life and of all other disciples is threaded together by the love of Jesus.

What will you learn?

Our Church's history has been woven with developments and declines throughout the past twenty centuries. With the aid of an ongoing timeline, you will come to understand the general theme of each time period as well as the important events and people.

The following outline gives you a brief overview of what you will be learning as the story of our Church unfolds.

14–476 C.E.
- Birth of the Church
- Beginning of the persecutions of Christians
- Destruction of the Temple in Jerusalem
- Division of the Roman Empire into eastern and western parts
- Fall of Rome to the northern tribes

476–800 C.E.
- Official end of the Roman Empire
- Beginning of the Muslim religion
- Rise in the great monastic orders and monasteries
- Establishment of the Holy Roman Empire
- Life of Saint Augustine

800–1400 C.E.
- Struggles between the kings and the popes for control of the people's loyalty
- Break between the Church in the East and the Church in the West
- Crusades against the Muslims
- Building of great cathedrals
- Age of scholars
- The Black Plague
- Life of Saint Francis of Assisi

1400–1700 C.E.
- Explosion of learning in the arts, sciences, and world exploration
- Martin Luther's challenges to the Catholic Church—origin of Protestant Churches
- Muslim Turks conquer Constantinople
- Council of Trent

1700–1900 C.E.
- Beginning of democratic governments
- Rise in secularism
- Age of Revolutions: American Revolution and French Revolution

1900 C.E.–Today
- Russian Revolution
- Second Vatican Council
- Advances in medical and scientific technology
- Rise in ecumenism

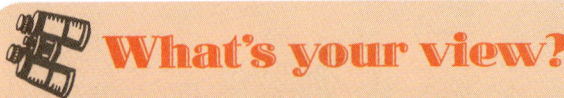

What's your view?

It is important to know our history as a people. Choose one of the following events that interests you. In a small group, share your view on how this event influenced the entire world.

- Vietnam War
- End of slavery in America
- Establishment of the thirteen colonies
- First landing on the moon
- Collapse of the Berlin Wall
- Invention of electricity
- Industrial Revolution
- John F. Kennedy's assassination

We have gifts that differ according to the grace given to us: prophecy, in proportion to faith; ministry, in ministering; the teacher, in teaching; the exhorter, in exhortation; the giver, in generosity; the leader, in diligence; the compassionate, in cheerfulness (Romans 12:6–8).

Each of us is called to serve our community. Briefly discuss ways that young people today can perform these services.

God has given me so many gifts. This is one way I can use my special gifts to serve the people in my community this week:
_____
_____

8

Pause to Pray

Leader: Jesus, we know your love is the common thread running throughout the history of our Church. As we learn the story of our community, help us see how our lives are part of the ongoing history.

Reader: Help us see how our Church community interacts with our society. We pray . . .

All: Jesus, hear us.

Reader: Help us grow in our own spiritual lives. We pray . . .

All: Jesus, hear us.

Reader: Help us carry on the message of the gospel. We pray . . .

All: Jesus, hear us.

Reader: Help us carry out our mission as your disciples. We pray . . .

All: Jesus, hear us.

Reader: Help us appreciate how our community is organized and run. We pray . . .

All: Jesus, hear us.

Leader: "Blessed be the God and Father of our Lord Jesus Christ! By his great mercy he has given us a new birth into a living hope through the resurrection of Jesus Christ from the dead, and into an inheritance that is imperishable, undefiled, and unfading, kept in heaven for you, who are being protected by the power of God through faith for a salvation ready to be revealed in the last time" (1 Peter 1:3–5).

HOMEWORK

The story of Jesus' life has much to teach us. For each of the following Scripture excerpts, write what event happened in Jesus' life, and then write one lesson you can learn from the story.

Scripture	What happened?	What can I learn?
Matthew 4:1–11		
Matthew 26:47–50		
Mark 4:35–41		
Luke 2:41–52		
John 2:1–11		

THE FIRST HUNDRED YEARS—
33–100 C.E.

Happy Birthday

In approximately 33 C.E., the first Pentecost, the birth of the Church, took place. Now suppose you and your group are in charge of planning a birthday party for the Church next Pentecost. Here are some questions to answer to help you plan the party. Once everyone has finished, compare your answers with those of the other groups in your class.

1. How old will the Church be next Pentecost?

2. What would make a good birthday hymn or song to sing at the party?

3. What would be some appropriate decorations?

4. What gift could your group give to the Church?

5. What words would you like to put on the birthday cake?

---

33 C.E. The crucifixion of Jesus; Pentecost—the birth of the Church

39 C.E. Christianity established in Antioch, an ancient city of Syria

45 C.E. Christianity established in Asia Minor

47–59 C.E. Paul traveled on four missionary journeys to spread the gospel

The Church's birthday

Pentecost, the fiftieth day after Easter, is considered the birthday of the Church. On this day in about 33 C.E., Jesus sent his Spirit upon the community of disciples gathered in Jerusalem. The Spirit transformed this frightened little group into joyful and courageous disciples dedicated to telling the good news about Jesus and about the salvation Jesus won for us through his resurrection.

When we say the Church started as a little community, we mean *little*—a couple hundred people at most. These Jewish people lived in an isolated area of the great Roman Empire. The good news they were eager to share was the story of a carpenter's son who was executed on a cross a few weeks earlier.

The odds were against them as they went to spread their message. Yet, through courage and perseverance, this little community expanded its influence to all parts of the known world by the end of the century.

Catechism Connection

The Church was made manifest to the world on the day of Pentecost by the outpouring of the Holy Spirit. [Cf. *SC* 6; *LG* 2.] . . . (1076)

Dialogue Corner

World peace can happen if everyone performs random acts of kindness.

You have been asked to spread this message to all people today.

- How would you go about doing this?
- How would you get people's attention?
- Who do you think it would be most difficult to get to listen?

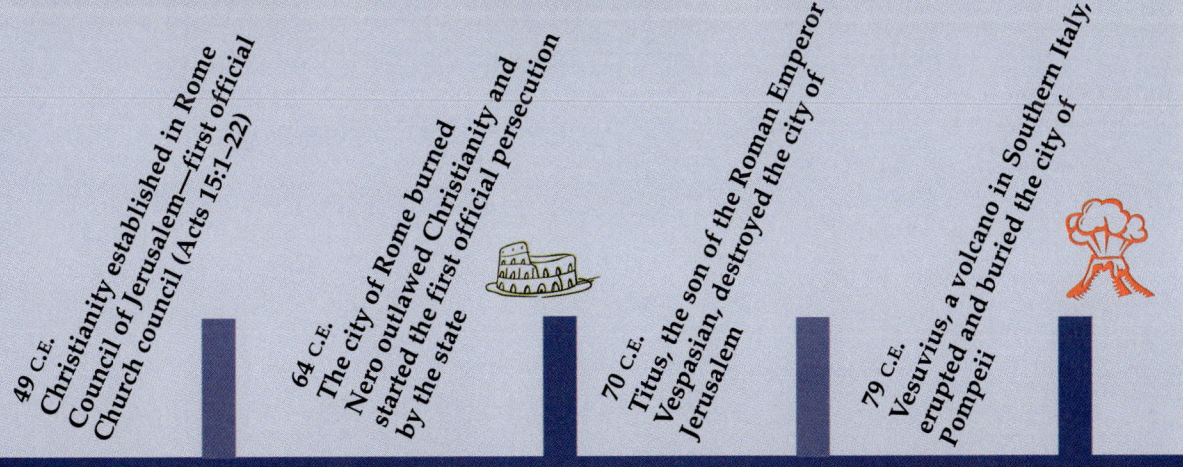

49 C.E. Christianity established in Rome — first official Council of Jerusalem — first official Church council (Acts 15:1–22)

64 C.E. The city of Rome burned — Nero outlawed Christianity and started the first official persecution by the state

70 C.E. Titus, the son of the Roman Emperor Vespasian, destroyed the city of Jerusalem

79 C.E. Vesuvius, a volcano in Southern Italy, erupted and buried the city of Pompeii

THE COMMUNITY'S INTERACTION WITH SOCIETY AND GOVERNMENT

The Roman Empire

When the Church was beginning to organize in the world, *world* meant the Roman Empire. This area included all of what we presently call Europe, North Africa, and the Near East. As big as the Roman Empire was, people could travel on good roads or on sailing ships from one area to another in safety. People could even send letters across the region and expect them to arrive at the correct location.

This empire included many different countries and tribes, over one hundred altogether. Each had its own language, customs, religions, and gods. Despite the many languages, people could communicate with each other because most spoke Greek or Latin as a second language. And in all the countries of the Roman Empire, there was a common law and justice system. But most importantly, this period was a time of peace. Roman armies controlled the land, and the people followed the laws of the empire.

Although the smooth travel, common language, and peaceful order made it easier for the Church to spread its message and mission throughout the Roman Empire during the first century, this period of time was not totally free from obstacles and troubles.

 TRIVIA TEASER

Romans are perhaps most famous for their engineering skills. Two thousand years ago, many wealthy Romans enjoyed the comforts of indoor plumbing and central heating in their homes. Some of the earliest roads built by the Romans are still in existence today.

Not a popular message

During this era, many of the people in the Roman Empire were living immoral lifestyles. The larger cities, where the disciples would try to form communities, were especially corrupt. Slavery was common. Sexual and social morality was at a low. And for entertainment, people would go to an arena to watch human gladiators kill each other.

Imagine walking into such a city and preaching love, purity, concern for those who were poor and weak, and the need to turn one's life over to God. The society at this time wasn't exactly in the mood to hear that kind of message. The idea of forming faith communities around the teachings of Jesus was contrary to just about everything people thought was important in the first century.

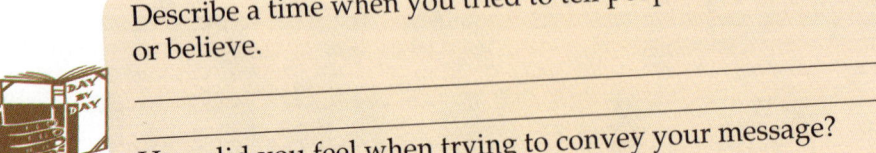

Describe a time when you tried to tell people something they didn't want to hear or believe.

How did you feel when trying to convey your message?

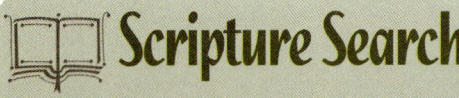 Scripture Search

Saint Paul describes the situation at this time in Romans 1:18–32. List at least ten evils that he saw happening within the Roman Empire.

1.
2.
3.
4.
5.
6.
7.
8.
9.
10.

Paul sums up his observations of many people in Roman society by saying, "They know God's decree, that those who practice such things deserve to die—yet they not only do them but even applaud others who practice them" (Romans 1:32).

The beginning of the persecutions

Despite people's corrupt lifestyles, the real challenge to the Church came from persecutions. The first people to persecute the disciples of Jesus were Jews who saw Christianity as a direct threat to their religion. Even Saint Paul had helped carry out such persecutions until his own conversion.

Surprisingly, the Roman Empire allowed for freedom of religion. People could practice any religion they wanted, provided it didn't violate basic laws and didn't stir up rebellion against the government and the emperor. Even the Jewish religion was legal. At first, Rome considered Christianity to be just a variation of the Jewish religion and left it alone.

But beginning in 64 C.E., the emperor Nero outlawed Christianity and started the first official persecution by the state. From that time until 313 C.E., to be a Christian was to be an outlaw and an enemy of the state. In these early days, the disciples of Jesus risked their lives when they chose to be a Christian. That says a lot about the courage and dedication of our first ancestors in faith.

TRIVIA TEASER

When Nero was persecuting the first Christians, he once gave a party during which he lit up the garden by using Christians as human torches. He had them hung on poles, covered with tar, and set on fire.

THE COMMUNITY'S SPIRITUAL LIFE

Conversion

Several key ideas will help you understand what it was like to be a disciple of Jesus in the early years of the Church. The first important factor is conversion. Roman Empire society included a great amount of corruption during this time. Many people lived totally contrary to the message of Jesus. For such people, to become a disciple of Jesus meant "sacrificing" one's entire past life. It usually meant giving up their lifestyle—friends, family, religion, and maybe even their work. And this was before Christianity was outlawed. After 64 C.E., becoming Christian may have meant giving up their lives, often in a most painful death.

When these early disciples first heard about Jesus and experienced his call to faith and friendship, they faced some tough decisions. Choosing to be a disciple wasn't like joining a club or taking up a hobby. It meant turning one's whole life around, a total conversion. It meant giving up a previous lifestyle and making the message of Jesus the very center of one's life. When it comes to role models to follow today, these people are heroes and heroines!

TRIVIA TEASER

Saint Stephen, the first Christian martyr, was stoned to death. Aptly enough, he is the patron saint to whom some people pray when they have headaches.

Community

Jesus' message about how to live is to love, care for, and support one another. The single most important thing Jesus asks us to do in terms of worship is to gather as a community and share the Eucharistic meal together. According to Jesus, leaders in his community are those who serve the rest. Jesus says it is the duty of the community to help anyone in the community who lacks food, clothing, or anything else.

Just a nice idea? The fact is, the early Christians actually tried to live that way. The Acts of the Apostles and Paul's letters make this clear. For our first ancestors, "being Christian" and "being community" were the same thing. They centered their lives on weekly Eucharistic gatherings. They would hear the word of God, take up collections for those in need, pray over the sick, and celebrate the Eucharist.

During the rest of the week, community members would be alert to help one another, visit the sick and those in jail, share their homes and their tables with travelers, and gather as families to pray and read the Scriptures. Christians did all these actions in addition to making a living and being a part of the greater society.

Once the persecutions began, the community members did all they could to protect one another. An underground system was developed with the use of coded messages to let one another know where and when the community was going to gather for Eucharist. And when community members were arrested, the community did all it could spiritually and physically to help them endure their trials and remain faithful to Jesus—even if it meant death. In those early days, being a community was more than responding to Jesus' command to love one another. In the era of persecutions, it was the key to survival for the Church.

Courage

The last key to understanding our first ancestors is their courage. It obviously took a great deal of courage to be a Christian in those days, because it sometimes meant torture and death. But there was another kind of courage these first disciples needed. Remember, even when there were no persecutions, society was not an easy place for a Christian to live. There were pressures everywhere to "do like the Romans do," which to some people meant to give in to sinfulness and evil—drunkenness, gluttony, cheating, lying, and sexual immorality.

Remember also that many of our ancestors in faith had once lived corrupt lives before they experienced their conversion to Jesus. Remaining morally "sober" in a hostile society (especially if you had once lived a corrupt life) took great courage—heroic courage in many cases.

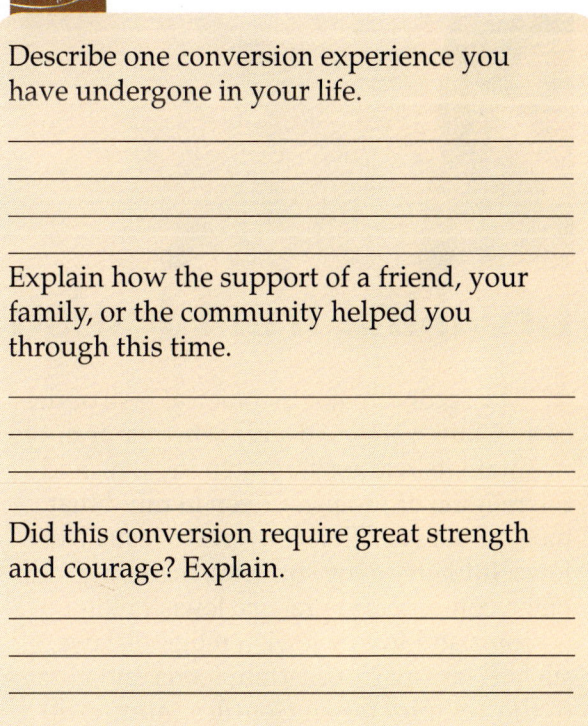

Describe one conversion experience you have undergone in your life.
_____
_____
_____
_____

Explain how the support of a friend, your family, or the community helped you through this time.
_____
_____
_____
_____
_____

Did this conversion require great strength and courage? Explain.
_____
_____
_____
_____
_____

THE COMMUNITY'S UNDERSTANDING OF THE GOSPEL MESSAGE

Gathering the stories and teachings of Jesus

When the Church first began its adventure, there was no written gospel. Instead, the community shared the stories and the memories of the apostles and other people who had known Jesus personally. Throughout the first century, the Gospels gradually developed into the four books we have today. The first major theological task of the Church was to gather these stories and teachings of Jesus so that all future disciples would have an accurate understanding of what Jesus had said and done.

Many of the letters that Peter, Paul, and other apostles sent to early communities were written before the Gospels. These letters represent the earliest theology of the Church. Those letters that were saved and made part of the New Testament served as the foundation for generations of disciples. Paul's letters have been especially helpful to Christians. He helped the first Christians—and us—discover the deeper meanings contained in the life and teachings of Jesus.

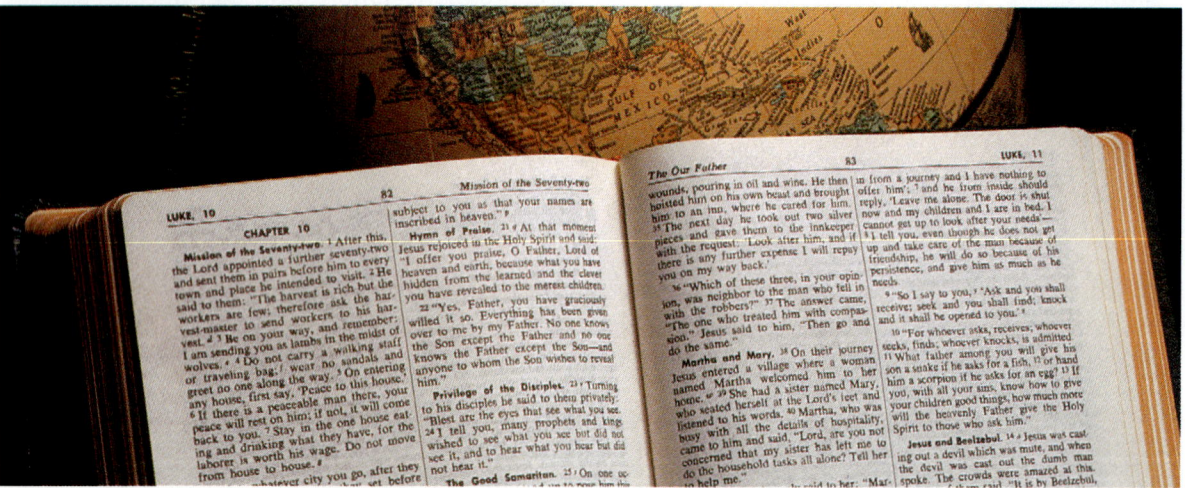

Breaking from Jewish Law

The second major theological task of the early Church was to decide whether or not to maintain its relationship with the Law and the religion of Judaism. Keep in mind that most of the very first converts to Jesus were Jews. Initially many converts, including Peter, continued to practice Jewish religious customs and follow Jewish religious laws, such as fasting from certain foods and going to the Temple. When Gentiles (non-Jews) wanted to join the Church, they were expected to be circumcised and to follow Jewish customs.

Paul began to take the message of Jesus to the people outside of Palestine. As he preached with great success, Paul formed the opinion that it wasn't fair to the Gentiles that they had to follow all the Jewish laws. His opinion created unrest in the Church, especially among Jewish converts. Turmoil over this issue was one of the reasons that led to the persecution of Christians by Jews who had not converted. Eventually, the Church adopted Paul's approach. But it wasn't until Rome destroyed Jerusalem and the Temple in 70 C.E. that Christianity really separated from Judaism.

THE COMMUNITY'S MISSION

Converting Jews, then Gentiles

When the apostles first started proclaiming the gospel to their fellow Jews in Palestine, Jerusalem was their center. At that time, James the Elder was the bishop of the community in Jerusalem, leaving Peter free to travel around to spread Jesus' message. Even when the disciples began to travel outside Palestine, they would usually preach to the Jewish communities throughout the Roman Empire.

But when some of the Jews began to persecute Christian converts, many of the disciples fled Jerusalem and Palestine. This actually helped spread the message of Jesus rather than suppress it. When many Jews outside of Palestine also resisted the Christian message, the Christians turned their focus to converting the Gentiles. Paul was the first to do this on a large scale. So by the end of the first century, especially after the destruction of Jerusalem, almost all preaching by the Christians was directed toward the Gentiles.

Willing to listen

The disciples soon discovered that the good news appealed most to those who were poor and the outcasts of Roman society, much as it did during the time of Jesus. The good news gave these people hope in a society that ignored and abused them. It gave them a sense of dignity and self-worth. But most importantly, the message the disciples preached promised them a place in the reign of God and everlasting life and happiness with Jesus—peace to people who had not known peace before.

Many of the first converts to Christianity were enslaved persons, laborers, widows, elderly people, social outcasts, and sinners. But eventually the gospel reached the hearts of just about every class of people. Rich nobles, officers in the army, and people who held positions in the court of the emperor also became Christians.

When a community gathered for Eucharist, you'd find nobles sharing the cup with beggars. Soldiers would help enslaved people collect food for those who were hungry. Greeks, Jews, Romans, Egyptians, and Persians would all sit at the same table. This sign of the kingdom could happen only through the grace of God and the action of the Holy Spirit.

Dialogue Corner

Who is my neighbor?
Read the parable of the good Samaritan in Luke 10:29–37. With a partner, rewrite the story, using a situation that you might encounter today. Then share your story with the class.

To the ends of the earth

We know that the disciples formed communities in every major city of the Roman Empire by the end of the first century. This growth took place despite a number of persecutions by the state. Rome, the center of the empire, became the center of the Church.

What we don't know is how far beyond the Roman Empire our ancestors in faith carried the gospel message in the first century. There are legends, for example, that Saint Thomas (the doubting Thomas of the Gospel) actually reached the southern tip of India. Other legends tell us the gospel message was carried as far as China. This may or may not be true, but we do know that the first disciples took Jesus' command to preach to all nations very seriously.

Scripture Search

Read the description of the early Church given in Acts 2:42–47. Using the four main activities of the Church described in the passage, write one example of how you see your parish carrying out these tasks today.

1. Faithful to the teachings of the apostles

2. Community life, support for each other

3. Celebrating Eucharist

4. Prayer

THE COMMUNITY'S ORGANIZATION

Charisms

To learn about how the early Church was organized, we need to examine three factors. The first factor was the use of charisms in the Church. *Charism* is a Greek word meaning "gift" or "talent." In the beginning, the Church was organized to a large extent around the gifts and talents of the disciples. Each disciple was blessed with a unique combination of charisms from the Holy Spirit that made that person and his or her mission special. Saint Paul explains it like this:

And God has appointed in the church first apostles, second prophets, third teachers; then deeds of power, then gifts of healing, forms of assistance, forms of leadership, various kinds of tongues (1 Corinthians 12:28).

In other words, whenever there was a need in the community, the situation was handled by the person who seemed to have the special gift for treating that need. It wasn't so much a question of education, wealth, or popularity. It was simply a matter of deciding whom the Spirit was calling to do a particular task. For the Church, it was clear that the Spirit was—and still is—the real authority and organizer for the community.

Ordination

Ordination was the second important factor in the early Church's organization. Some people were chosen and anointed to share in the priesthood of Jesus in a special way, just as the apostles had been selected. Very early on the Church established standards for these people who were ordained to serve their community. Here are some of the things Paul says about this to help guide Timothy, one of the bishops Paul ordained:

Now a bishop must be above reproach, married only once, temperate, sensible, respectable, hospitable, an apt teacher, not a drunkard, not violent but gentle, not quarrelsome, and not a lover of money.

Deacons likewise must be serious, not double-tongued, not indulging in much wine, not greedy for money; they must hold fast to the mystery of the faith with a clear conscience. And let them first be tested; then, if they prove themselves blameless, let them serve as deacons (1 Timothy 2–3, 8–10).

The Church early on organized with rules, duties, and a body of truths. The foundation for organizing the Church was solid. This solid foundation was the apostles, whose work carried on the mission of Jesus.

The great debate

The third key factor in the organization of the Church in the first century was the way it resolved its first major debate. Remember how Peter and many of the first Christians felt Gentiles should follow Jewish laws? And how Paul opposed the idea? This very important problem needed to be resolved before it destroyed the unity of the Church. To solve the problem, all the apostles and other elders in the Church held a meeting in Jerusalem in 49 C.E. They discussed, they argued, and they prayed to the Spirit for guidance. Finally, Peter and the other apostles accepted Paul's position. It became official policy that Gentiles did not have to follow Jewish religious customs. That meeting in Jerusalem is now called the *Council of Jerusalem*.

The reason this debate is so important is that it established the process that the Church has followed ever since to decide its problems of doctrine. In the future, the Church would form other councils to address other problems. The formation of these councils is one of the reasons the Church has been able to maintain its unity and preserve the teachings of Jesus. Councils are one part of the magisterium, or teaching office, of the Church.

Have you met . . . *Paul, Apostle to the Gentiles*

Probably no one person played a greater role in promoting the Church in the early years after Jesus' death and resurrection than Paul. He was about twenty-four when Jesus was crucified in 33 C.E. A devout, well-educated Jew, Paul belonged to the same Pharisee sect to which some of the people who had given Jesus such a hard time during his preaching days belonged. Paul was a loyal and devoted Jew, so loyal that he was one of the leaders in the persecutions against the followers of Jesus. Paul was frequently called Saul, his Hebrew name.

In fact, Paul was on his way to arrest some Christians when he had his famous conversion experience (Acts 9:1–22). After his conversion, Paul used his many talents and his great energy to help spread the very faith he had first tried to suppress. In the process, Paul traveled throughout Greece and Asia Minor on four different missionary journeys, establishing Christian communities in several major cities. He wrote numerous letters to these communities after he left them, encouraging, instructing, and correcting the new converts. In a letter to the Christians in Corinth, Paul told of the many struggles he endured while traveling on his missionary journeys.

Five times have I received from the Jews the forty lashes minus one. Three times I was beaten with rods. Once I received a stoning. Three times I was shipwrecked; for a night and a day I was adrift at sea; on frequent journeys, in danger from rivers, danger from bandits, danger from my own people, danger from Gentiles, danger in the city, danger in the wilderness, danger at sea, danger from false brothers and sisters; in toil and hardship, through many a sleepless night, hungry and thirsty, often without food, cold and naked (2 Corinthians 11:24–27).

Besides being brave, tough, and full of energy, Paul was a passionate man. He loved deeply and tenderly those he brought to faith in Jesus. He loved Jesus with his whole being. But he could also turn all that energy and passion against anyone who tried to lead others away from Jesus.

Paul was executed in Rome during the persecution of Nero around 65 C.E. Tradition tells us that he died on the same day Peter died. This is why, from the earliest days of the Church, the feast of Peter and Paul has been celebrated together.

 What's your view?

Share your views about the following questions with a partner or in a small group. Explain.
- Who, if anyone, is persecuting the Church today?
- Are people dying for their faith today? Who? Where?
- Are there any another kinds of persecution other than physical persecution?

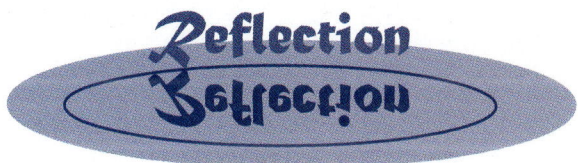

They devoted themselves to the apostles' teaching and fellowship, to the breaking of bread and the prayers (Acts 2:42).

Briefly discuss how we experience community in the Church today. How do we experience the aspects of community described in this passage from the Acts of the Apostles?

This is one way I help teach others in my community:
_____
_____

This is one way I serve as a member of the Church family:
_____
_____

This is one way I experience Eucharist with my community:
_____
_____

Pause to Pray

Leader: We listen now to the story of Saul's conversion. (Read aloud Acts 9:1–22 in your Bible.)
Reader: For the courage to change what needs to be changed in us. We pray . . .
All: Lord, help us.
Reader: For the ability to choose right over wrong. We pray . . .
All: Lord, help us.
Reader: For the times we fail to follow the teachings of Jesus. We pray . . .
All: Lord, help us.
Reader: For the ability to thank the people who have shown us the way to follow our faith. We pray . . .
All: Lord, help us.
All: Lord, thank you for the times of conversion in our own lives. We ask you to be with us as we continue to make decisions as Christians. Help us do our best in following your example. Amen.

HOMEWORK

In the early Church, miracles seemed to play a major role in helping promote faith in the gospel. Read Acts 9:32–43 and write out your answers to the following questions.

What miracles were performed? By whom?
_____
_____
_____

Do you think we still need miracles to spread the faith? Why or why not?
_____
_____
_____

What kinds of miracles happen today? Explain.
_____
_____
_____

What is one miracle you have experienced in your own life?
_____
_____
_____

THE COURAGE TO BE CHRISTIAN—100-312 C.E.

If people only watched your words and actions, would they be able to tell you're a Catholic Christian? Answer the following questions with a specific example from your own life to see how you live a Christian life.

1. Do you take time to pray in the morning? _____ Before bed? _____
My example: _____

2. Do you pray before meals? _____
My example: _____

3. Have you stood up for someone being put down? _____
My example: _____

4. Have you given of your time to help someone in need? _____
My example: _____

5. Do you attend Mass every Sunday? _____
My example: _____

6. Do you participate in Mass by singing and saying the prayers? _____
My example: _____

7. Have you forgiven someone who has hurt you? _____
My example: _____

8. Have you obeyed your parents and teachers? _____
My example: _____

9. Do you willingly admit you are a Catholic? _____
My example: _____

10. Do you set a good example for those younger than you? _____
My example: _____

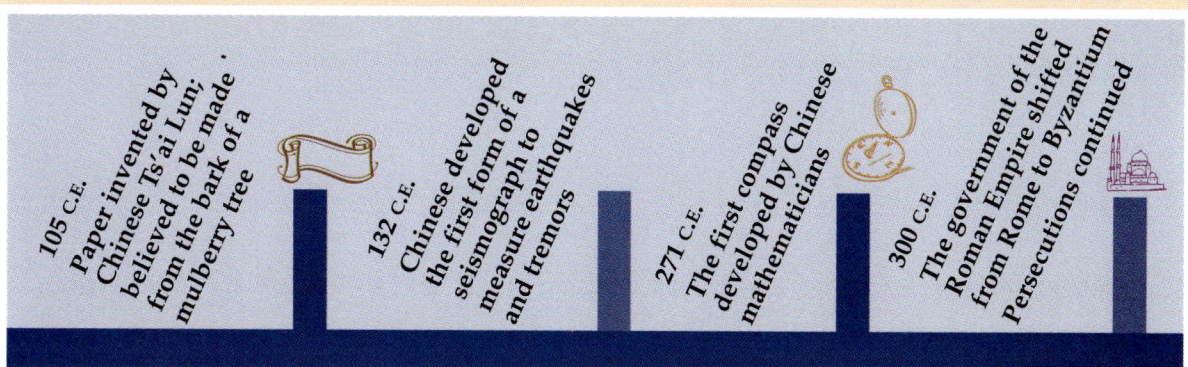

105 C.E. Paper invented by Chinese Ts'ai Lun; believed to be made from the bark of a mulberry tree

132 C.E. Chinese developed the first form of a seismograph to measure earthquakes and tremors

271 C.E. The first compass developed by Chinese mathematicians

300 C.E. The government of the Roman Empire shifted from Rome to Byzantium Persecutions continued

Changes in the Christian life

As you now know, there was a great deal of excitement and energy in the Church during its first seventy years. Eyewitnesses to the life of Jesus, including some of the apostles, were still alive. The power of the Holy Spirit seemed to be everywhere. Miracles were common aids to conversion. And many Christians, including Saint Paul, believed for a time that Jesus' return was just about to happen—and with it, the end of the world. Don't take this wrong, though. Being Christian in the first century was not always easy. Many people suffered persecutions during this time.

The period 100–312 C.E. saw some changes in the Christian life. The apostles and other eyewitnesses of Jesus were no longer living. The belief that Jesus would return any day now was becoming less and less common. And the persecutions begun by Nero continued off and on for the next 250 years. This time was probably the single, toughest period the Church ever faced. It took real courage to be Christian.

What is the most courageous thing you've ever had to do because of your faith in Jesus? Explain.

THE COMMUNITY'S INTERACTION WITH SOCIETY AND GOVERNMENT

Willing to worship the emperor?

A major reason the Roman Empire continued to persecute Christians was more political than religious. The Romans conquered many countries that had nothing in common with them. To maintain the loyalty of these people to the empire, the Romans often required them to worship the Roman emperor. From the time of Augustus, each new Roman emperor was considered a god. The Jews were one group not held to this. The requirement was not a problem for other groups who worshiped many gods. Adding the emperor to their list of gods did not betray their religious beliefs.

But worshiping the emperor was a problem for Christians once they were no longer seen as a faction of Judaism. They believed in only one all-powerful God. To worship the emperor meant to reject their faith in Jesus. In good conscience they couldn't worship the emperor or offer the required sacrifices to him. You can see the problem. To be a Christian meant you were a traitor and an enemy of Rome.

What's your view?

What kinds of gods do you see people worshiping in the world today? Share your thoughts with the class.

Christians are targets for anger

Another reason society and the government were so anti-Christian had to do with Rome's growing problems. From the middle of the first century, the empire began a slow decline. There was the general moral decay, but there were many other problems, too. The government had trouble raising money, so it kept increasing taxes. Unfortunately many people didn't have any work so they couldn't pay the taxes. And without money, there was no food, resulting in serious hunger. To make things worse, there was also a growing threat of invasions by northern tribes coming out of Germany and the East.

These and other problems kept getting worse from 100 C.E. until the fourth century. As the problems grew, people became frightened and angry. Christians made ideal targets for this anger because their faith forbade them to fight back or seek revenge. Superstitious people were convinced that the Roman gods were punishing Rome because the Christians refused to worship them. As the problems in the empire got worse, persecutions sprang up in various places.

Moving the government

One major change in society during this time was the gradual shift of the government from Rome to Constantinople. This shift was completed by 300 C.E. The empire was divided into an eastern and a western half, but the emperor had his court in the East at Constantinople (now Istanbul in modern Turkey). Great Rome gradually became a second-rate city. Many important people, with their wealth and riches, moved to the new capital.

The reasons for the shift in government were numerous. Despite it being a political move, this division in government eventually affected the Church as well. The effect on the Church will be discussed later.

TRIVIA TEASER

The official language of the Roman Empire was a form of Greek. Latin was considered the language of the common people, the vulgar language. It wasn't until Pope Victor I's reign from 189 to 199 C.E. that the Church in the West changed its official language from Greek to Latin.

THE COMMUNITY'S SPIRITUAL LIFE

The Age of Martyrs

This period is known as the *Age of Martyrs*. Martyrs are faithful witnesses who choose to suffer death rather than deny their religious beliefs. Every period of our Church history has had such people. The twentieth century saw people like Archbishop Oscar Romero become modern-day martyrs.

Have you met . . . *Archbishop Oscar Romero (1917–1980)*

Archbishop Oscar Romero of El Salvador was shot to death while saying Mass in San Salvador. During his time as archbishop, he had worked against injustices in this small country in Central America. Romero was angered by how landowners often unjustly treated the people who were poor. It was because of his beliefs and preaching that he was murdered.

Prior to his death, Archbishop Oscar Romero shared his thoughts about what it means to be willing to die for what you believe.

I have often been threatened with death. I must tell you, as a Christian, I do not believe in death without resurrection. If I am killed, I shall arise in the Salvadoran people. I say so without boasting, with the greatest humility.

Martyrdom is a grace of God that I do not believe I deserve. But if God accepts the sacrifice of my life, let my blood be a seed of freedom and the sign that hope will soon be reality. Let my death, if it is accepted by God, be for my people's liberation and as a witness of hope in the future.

You may say, if they succeed in killing me, that I pardon and bless those who do it. Would, indeed, that they might be convinced that they will waste their time. A bishop will die, but God's Church, which is the people, will never perish.

During the Age of Martyrs, persecution didn't always mean death. Although they may have been spared from death, many people did lose the lifestyle they had and the possessions they owned. Christians were forced to give up their homes when they were arrested and imprisoned. Some were sold into slavery and forced to work for the state for the rest of their lives. All their property was taken by the government.

When the penalty was death, Christians were sometimes tortured before their execution. Torture was used to get the Christians to reject Jesus and offer sacrifices to the emperor. Simply describing the acts of torture is enough to make a sane person cringe. Two very painful methods of torture included breaking all of the victim's teeth with a hammer and pulling out the Christian's fingernails with pincers. Sometimes torturers used whips, branding irons, knives, and needles to inflict pain. Death itself was no easier. People were burned alive, drowned in sacks filled with stones, crucified, dunked in boiling tar, or left naked to freeze on a lake of ice. And as you've probably heard, some Christians were placed in an arena with hungry lions. Given nothing with which to defend themselves, the Christians were eaten alive as Roman spectators watched.

Many people died in these ways. The only thing they would have had to do to avoid the excruciating torture and death was to say three simple words—"I reject Jesus." But very few did! Instead these heroes and heroines remained faithful witnesses even in the face of death.

TRIVIA TEASER

To be sentenced to work in the salt mines was considered a death penalty during this time. Miners worked and lived below the ground and never returned above ground. Few lived more than a year. Many Christians were condemned to the salt mines during the persecutions.

Scripture Search

Read 1 Peter 3:13–17.

1. Have you ever had to suffer for "being good"? Give an example.

_____

_____

_____

2. What is your "reason for hope"? How would you explain it to others?

_____

_____

_____

Women Saints

According to Scripture and tradition, women were a vital part of the development of the early Church. Many women and girls gave up their lives bravely for their beliefs. Some of these women are honored as saints. One such famous saint of the first century was Perpetua.

Perpetua was a young married woman with an infant son. According to her writings, she and five other catechumens were imprisoned. Her worst suffering while awaiting martyrdom came from the efforts of her father, who was not a Christian, to dissuade her. She said, "Father, do you see this vase?" When he replied yes, she continued, "Can it be named anything but what it really is? So I also cannot be called anything else than what I am, a Christian." Perpetua was eventually martyred in the arena in Carthage.

Two other women who testified to the power of the Spirit in their lives were Marcella and Paula. By the year 382 C.E., there was a thriving monastic community under Marcella's direction. Many women came to her house to engage in Scripture study, prayer, and the practices of asceticism (including giving money to those who were poor). Saint Jerome often lectured to these women, discussed the varied texts of Scripture, and recited the psalms with them. This group of women lived, in a different way and a different age, the original vision of the Christian message. Their lives were based on their love for Christ.

Between 386 and 389, Paula supervised the construction of two monasteries in Bethlehem, which were funded by her vast wealth. The men's monastery was finished first, and Paula's friend and mentor, Saint Jerome, moved in. Paula built her convent as close as she could to the Basilica of the Nativity, which had been erected on the site of Jesus' birth by another faith-filled woman, Helena.

Paula's monastery was divided into three sections, according to the different walks of life of the women. Here they lived, worked, and took their meals separately, but came together for prayer and worship. All dressed alike and no one owned anything except her clothing. Paula was the leader and managed her convents with skill and tact.

Keeping the faith alive

A few Christians openly and eagerly sought martyrdom. But these were the exception. The majority of our ancestors did all they could—short of denying Jesus—to stay alive and to spread the faith.

Safety and survival were key to Christian life in the Roman Empire. So for safety and survival, many Christians held secret meetings, usually late at night or early in the morning. They learned to use secret codes to tell other Christians when and where to meet. Often they hid a fellow Christian when the police were looking for that person. Many Christians fled for safety to other cities or other parts of the empire where there was no persecution at the time.

So they survived because of their secrecy and cooperation with one another. But more than anything, the Christians found strength and support in their Eucharistic celebrations. Here they would experience Jesus in their midst through the Bread of Life and Cup of Salvation and through the word of God that the leaders preached to them.

TRIVIA TEASER

The fish is a secret sign used by the early persecuted Christians to designate themselves as believers in Jesus. The initial letters of the Greek words for "Jesus Christ, God's Son, Savior," spell the Greek word for fish.

Honoring the saints

Our tradition of honoring saints developed during the Age of Martyrs. It was and is our belief that the martyrs went straight to heaven. This means they are now in a special position to pray for us. The early Christians realized this. They would gather the martyrs' remains and bury them reverently. They would ask these friends of theirs who had been martyred, especially those who had been exceptionally brave or holy, to intercede for them with God.

Our understanding of the communion of saints has its origin here. The practice of honoring the saints, asking for their intercession, and visiting shrines built in their honor comes from these early days and the great faith of our ancestors.

TRIVIA TEASER

Saint Apollonian, martyred in the year 249, had all her teeth knocked out after being hit in the face by a Christian persecutor. She is the patron of dental diseases and is often invoked by those with headaches.

Catechism Connection

Martyrdom is the supreme witness given to the truth of the faith: it means bearing witness even unto death. The martyr bears witness to Christ who died and rose, to whom he is united by charity.... (2473)

Turn to Appendix I: Saints for Our Time (pages 106–7). From this list, choose three saints whose stories interest you. Write a short prayer to each of them to help you grow stronger as a Catholic today.

Saint _____   Saint _____   Saint _____
Prayer: _____   Prayer: _____   Prayer: _____
_____   _____   _____
_____   _____   _____
_____   _____   _____

THE COMMUNITY'S UNDERSTANDING OF THE GOSPEL MESSAGE

Apologists and teachers

During this time, a number of our most learned ancestors tried to explain our faith to non-Christian leaders and philosophers of the time. Our ancestors hoped that if the leaders and philosophers understood the faith, they would stop fearing Christians and stop persecuting them as enemies of the state. Our ancestors also challenged Christians who tried to corrupt the teachings of the apostles.

We call these educated ancestors *apologists* and *Church fathers*. Apologists defended the faith through their lives and writings. They used their skills in philosophy and language to challenge the teachings of non-Christians. Two of the most famous apologists were Saint Justin Martyr and Saint Irenaeus of Lyons.

Church fathers were men of extraordinary faith who, through their teachings, gave hope and courage to the Christians of this time. Two of the most well-known Church fathers were Saint Ignatius of Antioch and Saint Polycarp of Smyrna.

We are fortunate that some of the writings, sermons, and speeches of the apologists and Church fathers have survived time. They help show how the faith of the apostles was handed down free of error in the next century. They also give us some of the knowledge we now have about what it was like to be a Christian back then.

TRIVIA TEASER

Saint Justin Martyr (100–165 C.E.) was beheaded during the reign of Emperor Marcus Aurelius when he refused to offer sacrifice to the Roman gods.

Fighting heresies

From the beginning, the apostles had to fight against heresies (false teachings about our faith) and misunderstandings about what Jesus actually taught. We know that both Peter and Paul often corrected errors that were spreading among their new converts. In every period, false teachings and false ideas sprung up in the Christian community.

In this period, two heresies the apologists challenged were Gnosticism and Montanism. *Gnosticism*, meaning "knowledge," was a mixture of eastern philosophy and religion. It stressed the spiritual side of life and claimed that everything physical and material was evil. Gnostics even denied that Jesus was truly human. This teaching returns again in future ages.

Montanism (named for its founder Montanus) taught that the second coming was imminent and that the world was about to end. Followers of this idea proposed a rigorous code of morality, including fasts and abstinences. This heresy denied the forgiveness of any sins committed after Baptism. Montanists caused a social conflict by denying the need for material goods and physical concerns (food, clothing, and shelter.

There is always just enough truth in such false teachings that they will appeal to some people. Too much stress on material goods and physical concerns is wrong. It is a good idea to be prepared for Jesus' return. But like all the other errors that we'll see through the centuries, what is missing is balance. The teachings of Jesus, who is both divine and human, are a delicate balance between spirit and matter, time and eternity, the recognition of human goodness and awareness of human evil.

So during these times of persecution, our ancestors had to work at keeping this balance and had to fight all the errors that rose within the Christian community. The bishops, apologists, and Church fathers did for Christians of this period what the apostles had done for the first converts. They kept the Christians centered on the gospel truths. Today our bishops and theologians help us keep this same kind of balance.

THE COMMUNITY'S MISSION

Rise in new converts

Another word for martyr is *witness*. Another term for witness is *good example*. It is a proof of God's power and wisdom that the persecutions Rome hoped would destroy Christianity actually helped spread it. For instance, the persecutions drew everyone's attention to the Christians. People who normally would have never heard about Jesus grew more curious. Everyone started talking about the Christians.

In other words, the persecutions gave Christianity a lot of publicity. But it was the witness or good example of the Christians when they faced torture and death that was the real force behind the spread of Christianity. Our Christian ancestors—especially the elderly and the children, whom you might expect to be weak and fearful—showed great faith and courage in the face of death. Such witness amazed many of the people who watched. It made them wonder about the mysterious power of this new religion. It also encouraged other Christians to be faithful until the end.

It was more than courage that amazed the onlookers. They couldn't believe how peaceful the Christians were in facing death or how ready they were to forgive those who were torturing them. They showed love and gentleness. This witness, too, got the onlookers interested in the Jesus the Christians followed. Who was he that he could gain such loyalty?

So even as Christians were being killed, new converts took their place. The greater the persecutions, the faster Christianity spread. That's a fact. It is also evidence of the power of God and the truth of the Church.

TRIVIA TEASER

The Roman Martyrology is a calendar listing of the martyrs who died on a given day. It often gives details of how the martyrs died. See if you can locate a copy. You may find it very interesting.

List three people, other than your parents or guardians, who have given you a good example and have helped you see what being a follower of Jesus really means.

_____
_____
_____
_____

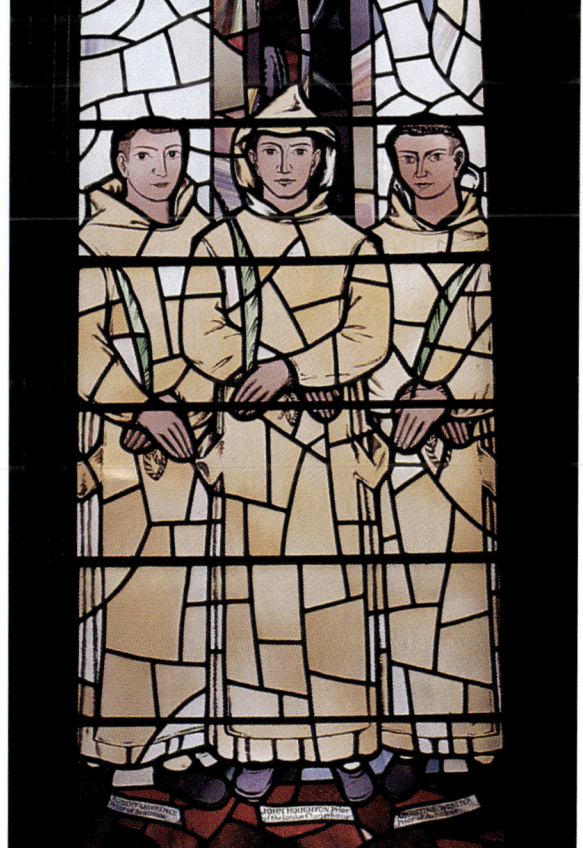

Spread of Christianity

By 300 C.E., Christianity was well-established in just about every part of the empire. When Christians would flee persecution in one part of the empire, they would bring the gospel to another part. Soldiers who had converted to Christianity would carry the gospel message wherever they traveled. Christians forced into slavery would spread the gospel among their fellow enslaved people and even to their masters.

In short, wherever you had a Christian, you had a missionary. Rome was still the spiritual center for Christians. But the Church itself spread to the farthest borders of the empire. We don't have any records of missionaries actually going beyond the empire to spread the gospel at this time, at least not in the organized way that would take place later. But within the empire, despite and because of the persecutions, the gospel was proclaimed and new converts continued to enter the Church.

THE COMMUNITY'S ORGANIZATION

Bishops, priests, and deacons

Building on the foundations laid by the apostles, the Church organized into local communities. Overseeing the community was the bishop. Local bishops had the same kind of authority that the apostles had. Besides caring for the faithful, they had the special task of seeing that no errors crept into the gospel message. Bishops were assisted by priests and deacons who cared for the people on a day-to-day basis. At this time, there were no Church laws forbidding bishops, priests, or deacons to marry. Many were married and had families. But even in this early period, some chose not to marry. They did this in imitation of Jesus, as a witness to the kingdom of God, and so they would have more freedom to serve the community.

In the time of the apostles, and for some time afterward, women held leadership positions along with men. Some served as deaconesses, for example. But because women seldom held leadership positions in society at that time, the Church did not allow them to hold the majority of the positions of authority.

Both the people and the official leaders remained active in carrying out the work of the Church. They brought the Eucharist to the sick and imprisoned. They cared for the poor. They taught new converts and tried to share their faith with their non-Christian neighbors. In those difficult early days, the mission of the Church was a real community effort, with all members helping out in any way they could.

Dialogue Corner

Share an example with the class of someone in your parish or community who you feel is active in carrying out the work of the Church.

The Bishop of Rome

The sense that Rome was the center for the Church and that the Bishop of Rome was the overall leader of the Church began with Peter. The central government the Church has today was still many years away; but even in these early days, it was clear to the people that the Bishop of Rome, the successor of Peter, held a special role in the Church and among all the other bishops. They did not use the title yet, but our ancestors knew that the Bishop of Rome was Jesus' visible representative on earth—a position later to be called *pope*.

TRIVIA TEASER

Almost all the popes during this period were martyred. They led as much by example as by word or authority. Saint Fabian, pope from 236–250 C.E., was the first victim of the persecution of Christians led by Roman emperor Decius. Ironically, during his pontificate, Fabian was responsible for appointing notaries to register the deeds of martyrs.

Scripture and creed

During this same period, the New Testament as we know it today was compiled. Originally, more than four Gospels were written. There were also numerous letters that were treated with great respect and seen as having great authority. So one of the tasks the Church carried out was to decide which writings should belong in the New Testament. This work continued until the fifth century.

During this same time, various creeds were being used. These were attempts to put the key beliefs handed down by Jesus and the apostles in a short form. Eventually one of these creeds, the Apostles' Creed, became the official and most widely used form. It isn't called the Apostles' Creed because the apostles wrote it. It's called the Apostles' Creed because our ancestors felt it best summarized all that the apostles taught the first Christians. It is still one of the best summaries of our faith ever written.

📖 Scripture Search

To help you become familiar with what is included in the New Testament, use a Bible to number the following books in the order in which they appear.

_____ Philemon	_____ 2 Timothy	_____ 2 Peter
_____ 1 Peter	_____ 2 John	_____ Jude
_____ Colossians	_____ 1 Corinthians	_____ Luke
_____ Acts of the Apostles	_____ Matthew	_____ 2 Corinthians
_____ Book of Revelation	_____ Philippians	_____ 2 Thessalonians
_____ Mark	_____ 3 John	_____ 1 Timothy
_____ John	_____ Romans	_____ Galatians
_____ Ephesians	_____ 1 Thessalonians	_____ 1 John
_____ Titus	_____ Hebrews	_____ James

I believe...

Complete the Apostles' Creed by filling in the correct words.

I [We] believe in _____ , the Father _____ , Creator of _____ and _____ ; I [We] believe in Jesus Christ, his only _____ , our Lord; he was _____ by the power of the _____ _____ , and born of the _____ Mary. He suffered under _____ _____ , was crucified, died, and was _____ .

He descended to the _____ . On the _____ day he rose again.

He ascended into _____ , and is seated at the _____ hand of the Father. He will come again to _____ the living and the dead.

I [We] believe in the Holy Spirit, the holy catholic _____ , the communion of _____ , the _____ of sins, the resurrection of the body and _____ everlasting. Amen.

Dialogue Corner

In a group of four, develop a short creed that states the most essential truths of the Catholic faith in thirty words or less. Share your creed with the other groups and decide which of the creeds best expresses your beliefs.

We believe:
_____
_____
_____
_____
_____
_____

Reflection

If you are reviled for the name of Christ, you are blessed, because the spirit of glory, which is the Spirit of God, is resting on you. Yet if any of you suffers as a Christian, do not consider it a disgrace, but glorify God because you bear this name (1 Peter 4:14, 16).

Briefly discuss how we can witness to our faith and help alleviate the suffering of fellow Christians.

Here are three ways I will witness this week to my faith in Jesus:
_____
_____
_____

Pause to Pray

Jesus,

Help me appreciate your real presence in the Eucharist as my ancestors did.

Help me follow in the footsteps of the martyrs and saints and be a witness to my faith by good example.

Help me be active in the work of your Church.

Amen.

HOMEWORK

Are you dressed as a Christian?

Read Ephesians 6:10–17. Write a list of the "armor" a Christian needs to be wearing when confronting evil. Then decide which one of these items young people today need the most and explain why.

The piece of armor young people need the most is _____

Young people need this item most because _____
_____
_____
_____
_____

FROM FREEDOM TO FEUDALISM—313–800 C.E.

A period of ups and downs

This period in our Church's history is like a roller-coaster ride. It begins with great news: Our ancestors finally receive freedom of religion and the persecutions come to an end. Then almost immediately the Church must battle for survival against heresies and false teachings that threaten to destroy it. About the time our ancestors conquer this problem, northern tribes overrun the Roman Empire, and civilization collapses. Gradually though, the Church converts the northern tribes. New kingdoms form to replace the Roman Empire and give some order to society. But peace doesn't last for long. The kings and princes of the new kingdoms try to take over the leadership of the Church from the pope and bishops. So hang on. You're in for a bumpy ride this chapter!

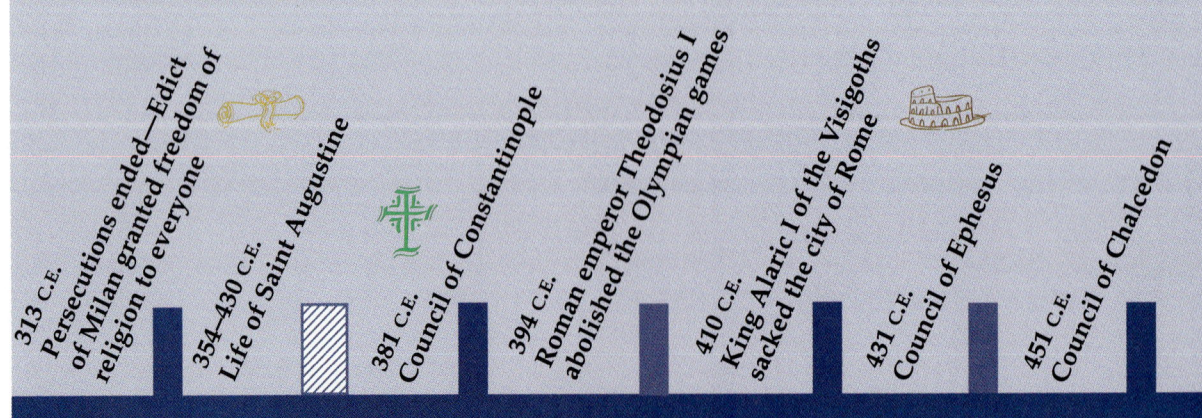

- 313 C.E. Persecutions ended—Edict of Milan granted freedom of religion to everyone
- 354–430 C.E. Life of Saint Augustine
- 381 C.E. Council of Constantinople
- 394 C.E. Roman emperor Theodosius I abolished the Olympian games
- 410 C.E. King Alaric I of the Visigoths sacked the city of Rome
- 431 C.E. Council of Ephesus
- 451 C.E. Council of Chalcedon

 **What's your view?**

The relationship between the Church and the state has a long history. Defining it is still an issue today. How do you feel about each of these Church and state issues we see in the headlines every day?

- Allowing prayer in public schools
  _____
  _____

- Tuition assistance for low-income families who want to send their children to private schools
  _____
  _____

- Using the phrase *In God we trust* on U.S. currency
  _____
  _____

- Allowing Christmas cribs or other religious symbols on public property
  _____
  _____

- Saying the phrase "under God" in the Pledge of Allegiance
  _____
  _____

Discuss your opinions with the other students in your class.

THE COMMUNITY'S INTERACTION WITH SOCIETY AND GOVERNMENT

The persecutions finally end!

For the first three hundred years of the Church's life, beginning with the execution of Jesus, Christians were persecuted. The persecutions finally ended when a general named Constantine became emperor of the Roman Empire. Constantine, along with his soldiers,

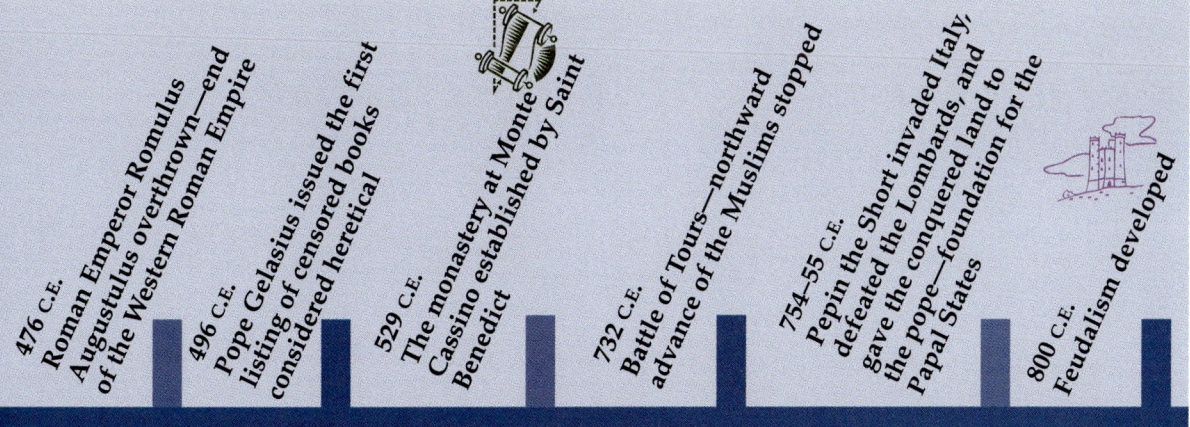

476 C.E. Roman Emperor Romulus Augustulus overthrown—end of the Western Roman Empire

496 C.E. Pope Gelasius issued the first listing of censored books considered heretical

529 C.E. The monastery at Monte Cassino established by Saint Benedict

732 C.E. Battle of Tours—northward advance of the Muslims stopped

754-55 C.E. Pepin the Short invaded Italy, defeated the Lombards, and gave the conquered land to the pope—foundation for the Papal States

800 C.E. Feudalism developed

battled fiercely against rival generals before he could take control of the empire. When he finally defeated his enemies, Constantine was convinced that the God of the Christians had helped him win the victory. As a result, Constantine, in one of his first official acts, issued the Edict of Milan in 313 C.E.

The Edict of Milan gave freedom of religion to everyone, including Christians, and it forbade any further persecution of Christians. The Christians could now worship together in public and openly preach the gospel without fear. Buildings confiscated by the government were returned, and churches could now be built.

Constantine's mother, Helena, had a great influence on her son. She was a convert to Christianity and helped her son understand the Church. Today, Helena is honored as a saint. Constantine himself wasn't baptized as a Christian until he was on his deathbed, but during his life he actively supported the Church. He helped it gain favor in a non-Christian society.

By the end of Constantine's reign in 337 C.E., the Church was firmly established as a part of society and the government. The Edict of Milan marks one of the major turning points in our history as Christians. We'll come back later to the effects all this had on the Church.

Scripture Search

Read Matthew 22:15–22. What do you think Jesus teaches us about the relationship between Church and state?

_____
_____
_____
_____

The decline and collapse of a civilization

In 313 C.E., the Roman Empire was still in relatively good shape. But northern tribes were on its borders waiting for a chance to invade. Alaric I, king of the Visigoths, had tried to invade Italy twice but was stopped both times by Roman general Flavius Stilicho. After Stilicho was executed, Alaric invaded Italy again in 410 C.E., capturing and sacking the city of Rome. At the time of the invasion, Pope Innocent I was away from Rome attempting to finalize a truce between Alaric I and Roman emperor Honorius.

Whenever the official government (the emperor and his armies) lost control in part of the empire, civilization in that area deteriorated. Education and the development of the arts stopped. Laws weren't enforced. Roads weren't maintained and public buildings crumbled. Pirates ruled the seas. Travel was dangerous, so trade and business broke down. People had no work and no money—and the government had no taxes. As Rome's great civilization unraveled in one area after another, problems multiplied.

First to fall apart was the government in the western part of the empire, in what is known today as Italy, France, Spain, England, and Ireland. By 700 C.E., the empire in the East also collapsed. With the fall of the governments in the East and the West, the Roman Empire no longer existed.

TRIVIA TEASER

While the Romans were clean shaven, the enemies who invaded the empire had beards. The Latin word for *beard* is *barbar*. Hence the invading enemies were called *barbarians*. Today we call any "uncivilized" person a barbarian.

Rise of feudalism

Imagine that our federal government suddenly collapses. There is no more Washington, D.C., no president, no Congress, and no Constitution. We no longer have armed forces, federal highways, or a postal system. Now imagine that each major city becomes a little kingdom all its own, with a king who rules with absolute power over the city, the surrounding towns, and the countryside. His word is law, and his army enforces that law. Whoever lives in his territory must work for, pay taxes to, and obey him.

This scenario is similar to what happened after the Roman Empire fell. It gives you an idea of what feudalism is and how it developed. The once unified Roman Empire with its powerful central government, common law, and common language was replaced with many small kingdoms. Each had its own ruler, its own laws, and eventually its own language. Without any sense of unity as a group, each small kingdom was always going to war to conquer its neighboring lands.

By 800 C.E. the great, powerful, unified Roman Empire was just a memory. In its place was a patchwork quilt of countries and kingdoms, each fighting the other for more power. This kind of disorganized, feudal society is where our ancestors had to worship, work, and live for the next 800 years. The effects such a society had on the Church and the effects the Church had on that society are still with us today.

The beginning of Islam

We hear a great deal today about Muslims and the religion of Islam, which began during this period in history. Muhammad (570–632 C.E.) was the founder of Islam. He grew up in Arabia, working first as a shepherd and later as a merchant. In his travels as a merchant, Muhammad became familiar with both the Jewish and Christian religions. One day he had a religious experience that convinced him he was called by the God of Abraham to be the final prophet sent by Allāh (his name for God). Muhammad believed Jesus was a great prophet, but not the Son of God.

In a very short time, Muhammad was able to convert many of his fellow Arabs to believe in Allāh, their one true God. Until then, Arabia had no central government. It was a collection of wandering tribes that fought constantly. Muhammad's religion gave the tribes unity. It also gave them a purpose. Muhammad taught that it was the duty of all Muslims to convert the infidel (anyone who did not believe in Allāh and his prophet, Muhammad).

By 650 C.E., the Muslims began to move out of Arabia. As they traveled, the Muslims waged a holy war along the eastern Mediterranean (the area of Palestine) and northern Africa. Because the Roman Empire that had ruled in those areas was no longer able to defend itself, the Muslims conquered country after country with ease. They even crossed over into Spain, conquered it, and moved up into what is now France. Finally, in 732 C.E., the Muslims were defeated in the famous Battle of Tours. That stopped their invasion—for the time being.

But by now, countries controlled by the Muslims and countries controlled by the Christians considered each other enemies. In the next 800 years, these two groups would battle each other many times. Often the Church was right in the middle of the fighting. Even today in some parts of the world, Christians and Muslims still see each other as bitter enemies.

TRIVIA TEASER

In just a little over 100 years from the founding of Islam, the Muslims had invaded and conquered one-third of the known world.

THE COMMUNITY'S SPIRITUAL LIFE

Keeping the faith

Constantine and other emperors who came after him began to show favor to the Christians. Ironically during these times, being a Christian could actually help you get a government position. Eventually, bishops and priests were made key officials in some parts of the empire and helped run the government.

This may sound good, but it also had a negative influence. Because of the favor to the Christians, many insincere people joined the Church in hopes of being appointed to the government by the emperor. These people had no real conversion; they were Christians only on the surface. They did not really know about Jesus, understand the gospel, or care about being disciples. Their membership tended to weaken the faith of the entire Church.

Even sincere Christians were inclined to take their faith more for granted. They were no longer challenged by persecutions. Therefore, keeping the faith alive was no longer their main concern. They were more caught up in worldly concerns and interests.

In general, then, the pure and fervent faith of earlier disciples lessened once it was both easy and popular to be called a Christian. Sure, there were still many holy, dedicated disciples in all the local faith communities, but the faith of the people was not as strong as it was in the earlier days of the persecutions.

TRIVIA TEASER

Gregorian chant was named after Pope Gregory the Great, who supported its development so the people could join in the singing at the Eucharistic celebrations. Chant eventually became the music used by monks when singing the psalms at prayer. It is still used today in some liturgies.

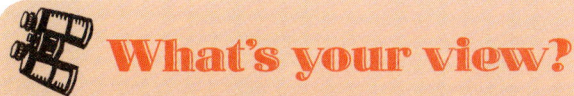

What's your view?

Read Matthew 10:5–15. What do you think would be the hardest part of being a disciple of Jesus during this time?

From the desert to the monastery

To balance this weakening of faith in the Church, the Spirit called forth a radical movement among its faithful. Christian men and women left their comfortable homes to go live in the desert or other uninhabited areas. There, they lived alone as hermits, spending their days and nights praying, fasting, and doing penance. This move to the desert actually started a century or so earlier. But once the persecutions ended, this type of lifestyle became much more popular.

Devout Christians living in the cities soon started traveling to visit these holy individuals to seek their prayers and their guidance. Some would decide to stay and live in solitude themselves. They would build a hut or find a cave and live as "disciples" of the holy individual. In some cases, little communities would form. These men and women would spend most of their time alone in prayer and fasting but would gather on Sunday or other times to celebrate the Eucharist together.

The monastic movement started as a result of these communities. One of the pioneers in starting monastic orders was Saint Benedict, who lived from approximately 480 to 550 C.E. He had been living as a hermit. But because of the numerous disciples who gathered around him, Saint Benedict decided to build a monastery at Monte Cassino in Italy. He then wrote a Rule that has served as a guide for monks to the present. At Monte Cassino the ideals of the desert (prayer, fasting, penance) were integrated with community life and community service. The phrase *pray and work* was Saint Benedict's motto for his followers.

In the western part of the world, Saint Benedict's Rule and his monastic style of "desert life" soon became the norm followed by all other monastic orders founded in later centuries. Saint Benedict's sister, Saint Scholastica, started a similar community for women near Monte Cassino. She used Benedict's Rule to guide the nuns. Soon, similar "desert" communities or monasteries for women began to form.

~ Peace and Quiet ~

What four aspects of living as a hermit or monk appeal to you?

1.

2.

3.

4.

Choose one aspect to share with the class and be prepared to explain why this appeals to you.

Describe a time when you needed to spend some time in solitude to think or pray.

How did you feel after taking this time for yourself?

Papyrus, an ancient form of paper, was plentiful when the Roman Empire was flourishing but became very scarce after the empire collapsed. People began to use *vellum*—dried skins of sheep and other animals—as a substitute. Many of the manuscripts the monks copied in the monasteries were written on vellum.

More than faith

Soon Benedictine monasteries were springing up all over Europe. A major responsibility of these monks and nuns was to keep the gospel ideals of Jesus alive within the Church. They were sometimes called *bloodless martyrs* because they sacrificed everything to live a solitary life of prayer and good works for Jesus.

But the monastic movement was very important for another reason. It became a shining light for the world during the collapse of the Roman Empire. The monks and nuns lived a consecrated life dedicated to God and to continuing the work of Jesus. They spent much of their time finding and preserving the ancient writings of the Romans and Greeks. They would copy these writings and then study them. These monasteries have served as a bridge between the ancient world and our world today. For the most part, what we know about Rome and Greece is due to thousands of dedicated monks and nuns who faithfully worked, wrote, and studied the ancient writings—out of love for Jesus.

Over time, the monasteries became little "centers of civilization." The monks cleared away swamps and reclaimed wastelands to build farms. They became experts in agriculture and raising cattle. Towns formed near the monasteries, and many people relied on the monks for employment and food. The abbot of the monastery was regarded in a similar way as a local mayor or governor. The monks started schools to teach children how to read and write. And on Sundays and feast days, the people gathered in the monastery church to celebrate the Eucharist.

In short, our faith-filled ancestors who fled society and went into solitude to dedicate themselves entirely to Jesus ended up shaping society more than most of the kings and princes of those days.

Dialogue Corner

Work together in a group of three to answer the following questions.

Many of today's religious communities have their roots in the monastic movement of this era. Name three religious communities that are active today.

1.
2.
3.

What are three "good works" today's religious communities carry out for the good of the Church and society?

1.
2.
3.

THE COMMUNITY'S UNDERSTANDING OF THE GOSPEL MESSAGE

A dangerous profession

Almost immediately after the persecutions ended, the Church faced another problem. False teachers, called *heretics*, began spreading errors, called *heresies*, among the faithful. Most of these errors had to do with Jesus. Some heresies claimed that Jesus was fully human but not really divine, not the Son of God. Other heresies taught the opposite—Jesus was fully divine but only appeared to be human. Still others said he was fully divine but only partially human.

Remember, there were no more eyewitnesses to the life of Jesus at this time. Thousands of newly-converted people—who had little or no previous knowledge about Jesus, the apostles, or Christian beliefs—were entering the Church. They could be misled easily.

Fortunately, some great saints and theologians were around. Though the debate was about theology, politics and power also had great influence. Some of our theologian-heroes, such as Athanasius, risked their lives to defend the faith. These theologians were sometimes kidnapped and held prisoner by supporters of the heretics. Mobs would riot to promote their particular heresy. As we have seen before, being a theologian and defender of the faith could be a dangerous profession.

Suppose you have recently met someone who wants to learn more about your friendship with Jesus. Write this person a letter explaining why you have chosen to be a disciple in our world today and how you go about doing this on a daily basis.

Dear _____ ,

_____
_____
_____
_____
_____
_____
_____

Yours truly,

_____

Age of councils

As you learned earlier, the apostles met in Jerusalem in 49 C.E. when there was a disagreement about what to do with Gentile converts. That meeting established a method to settle disputes and other theological questions. As time went on, the Church began to hold ecumenical councils. (*Ecumenical* here means "worldwide.") Bishops gathered from every place in the world where the Church was established. They would debate intensely, discuss, and pray over the dispute in question.

A decision would emerge from the meeting, most likely by a vote. Whatever was decided by the bishops and approved by the Bishop of Rome became the official teaching for all Christians throughout the world.

Three famous councils were held during this period. The first, the Council of Constantinople, was held in 381 C.E. This council accepted the Nicene Creed as the official statement of beliefs for our Church. We profess this creed on Sundays and at other important liturgies.

The Council of Ephesus was held in 431 C.E. Disputing two heresies, the Council of Ephesus clarified that Christ is true God and true man and that Mary is truly the Mother of God.

The third council held during this period was the Council of Chalcedon in 451 C.E. At this meeting, the bishops summarized and clarified previous councils by stating that Jesus was indeed fully human and fully divine.

Scripture Search

Read Matthew 16:13–20. Suppose someone told you that he or she didn't believe Jesus is the Son of God. What three reasons would you give to explain your own belief that Jesus is indeed the Son of God?

1. _____
   _____
2. _____
   _____
3. _____
   _____

Catechism Connection

"The college of bishops exercises power over the universal Church in a solemn manner in an ecumenical council." [CIC, can. 337§1.] But "there never is an ecumenical council which is not confirmed or at least recognized as such by Peter's successor." [*LG* 22.] (884)

Great theologians

Some of the greatest theologians of all time lived during this period of history. We can only list a few names here, even though each person deserves a whole chapter to tell his story. This was the era of Jerome, who first translated the Bible into common Latin; Pope Saint Leo the Great, who turned away Attila the Hun; Pope Gregory the Great, who brought order to the Church when civilization was collapsing; and Ambrose, the famous bishop of Milan.

Yet perhaps one man stands out above all the others of this period—Augustine (352–430 C.E.). One thing that makes Augustine so interesting is not just his famous writings in theology, but the fact that for much of his youth into his middle years, he wasn't even a Christian. He lived a sinful life. For fifteen years, Augustine lived with a mistress who bore him an illegitimate child.

His mother, Saint Monica, was a devout Christian who never gave up praying for his conversion. When it finally happened, Augustine turned all his talent and energy into learning about and then teaching the faith. Aside from Paul the apostle, perhaps no one has had more influence on our understanding of the gospel than Augustine.

TRIVIA TEASER

Jerome's translation of the Hebrew and Greek Bible into Latin, called the *Vulgate*, was intended for the common people. The name *Vulgate* derives from the Latin word *vulgar*, meaning "common."

THE COMMUNITY'S MISSION

Monks and missionaries

Two things happened that had a big influence on the spread of the gospel during this period. First, the Church suddenly found itself face-to-face with millions of people who had never heard of Jesus or the gospel. These people were part of huge tribes that had spent many years moving toward the empire from the East and the North. By the time they began to move into the empire itself, the Church was well established and was often considered part of the government. To "civilize" these people meant that they had to learn about Jesus. So in one sense, the Church did not have to go out looking for converts. They came looking for the empire and found the Church.

The second important factor in the spread of the gospel during this time was the role of the monks. Many monks, trained by years of prayer and study, felt called to leave the monasteries and journey as missionaries into faraway lands to bring Jesus' message to the people. At times, the pope or bishop would specifically ask the monks to travel and teach the gospel.

Christianity spread to many parts of Europe during this period, thanks to the efforts of dedicated missionaries. It was during this time that Saint Patrick traveled to Ireland and converted the people living there. Clovis, king of the Franks (the future French), and many of his subjects were baptized by Saint Remigius in 496 C.E. Saint Augustine of Canterbury, sent by Pope Gregory the Great, led the conversion of England in the sixth century. And Saints Willibrord and Boniface traveled north into the Germanic lands to spread the message of the gospel.

Almost immediately after hearing the gospel, the people of these foreign lands built new monasteries. Soon, the monks living in these monasteries began to travel to new lands as missionaries, too. So even as the Roman Empire was collapsing and being taken over by northern tribes, the Church in its own way was "conquering" its enemies and introducing them to Jesus.

Missionary Efforts

Fourth Century
Bishop Ulfilas converted the Visigoths

Around 450 C.E.
Saint Patrick converted the Irish

496 C.E.
Saint Remigius baptized Clovis and many of his Frankish followers

597 C.E.
Saint Augustine of Canterbury converted Anglo-Saxon England

740s C.E.
Then Englishman Boniface won many people from central Germany to Christ

Ninth Century C.E.
Saint Cyril and Saint Methodius, known as the *Apostles of the Slavs*, spread the gospel to Bohemia

THE COMMUNITY'S ORGANIZATION

The clergy and the laity

During the early days of the persecutions, the bishops and priests who served the community were for the most part "ordinary people." These ordinary people presided at the Eucharist and were the spiritual leaders and official teachers of the gospel. But in society itself, they had no special rank or authority; they lived and worked alongside the rest of the faithful in the community. Many were married and had families.

This situation changed once the government began to favor the Church. Church leaders, especially bishops, often became public officials, who were responsible for maintaining the law and order of the empire. Non-Christians and Christians alike were expected to show respect to and obey these public officials. As a display of reverence, the government gave the Church leaders places of honor at official functions and assigned soldiers and servants to assist them. One thing that was expected of the bishops was that they wear uniforms—official robes that represented their government rank.

In time, as the empire collapsed, the bishops and other priests became responsible for maintaining all duties of the government in a specific city or area. Usually, they would carry out their new duties very well, protecting the weak, caring for the poor, and maintaining some level of peace and order.

These new responsibilities did have a negative effect on the Church. Before long, there was a definite class distinction between the clergy (ordained bishops and priests) and the laity (people). The clergy became more distanced from the laity; they now had special titles, official garb, special privileges, and special civil powers. This division caused the laity to feel as if they were less important than the clergy in the eyes of the Church.

TRIVIA TEASER

Pope John I was the first pope to change his given name. The reason for the change was that his given name had been Mercury, the name of a Roman god. Ever since Pope John I changed his name in the sixth century, all popes have also taken a new name.

Feudal society, feudal Church

By the time the Roman Empire collapsed and feudal kingdoms emerged, bishops were considered princes and rulers in their own right. Thus the bishops and the Church became owners of large amounts of land. The people who lived in these areas paid taxes directly to the bishops. So to protect their land (and their investment), the bishops would sometimes hire armies to keep order.

As this was happening, monasteries were becoming centers of civilization, too. The abbot (head of the men's monastery) and abbess (head of the women's monastery) had basically as much power and authority as the bishops. They were not only responsible for the people of their monastery, but governed an entire area of people and towns.

In the process of governing these lands, the bishops and monasteries often became quite wealthy. Secular kings and princes viewed the districts governed by bishops and monasteries as "prizes." They would fight each other and fight the bishops and abbots to gain control of these "prizes."

A gap between the clergy and the laity

Meanwhile, after the collapse of the empire, most of the common people who had recently converted to Christianity were uneducated and unskilled. In the feudal society, these people became the peasant class. This class included a majority of the faithful, who depended on the educated ruling class of bishops, abbots, and abbesses not only for their growth in faith, but often for day-to-day survival.

So from the years 313 to 800 C.E., a huge gap began to grow, separating the powerful, educated, and often wealthy bishops (the clergy) from the poor, uneducated, faithful people (the laity).

Dialogue Corner

Gaps between two groups of people, like that of the clergy and the laity during this time period, are a common occurrence. What are some divisions that exist in the following areas today? Are these divisions negative or positive? For example, one division in government today is the differing political parties and their views on key issues, such as health care. This gap is negative because unless there is some agreement between the two parties, health care issues will remain unsolved.

- schools
- social classes
- families
- government
- Church
- peers

What do you believe about some of the faith issues mentioned in this chapter?

The human nature of Jesus

The divine nature of Jesus

Mary's role in the Church

The importance of personal prayer

Scripture Search

Read John 15:1–17. List three commands given by Jesus that all disciples are called to carry out in their lives.

1.

2.

3.

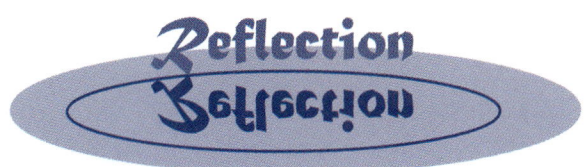

Reflection

In the morning, while it was still very dark, [Jesus] got up and went out to a deserted place, and there he prayed (Mark 1:35).

Briefly discuss ways that young people today can make time in their busy lives for prayer.

My favorite place to pray is _____

Right now in my life I need to pray for _____
_____

Pause to Pray

Jesus,
Help me find a "desert" place to pray where I can be quiet and peaceful.
Help me be respectful and obedient toward my parents and teachers.
Help me put God's will for me above my own selfish wishes.
Amen.

HOMEWORK

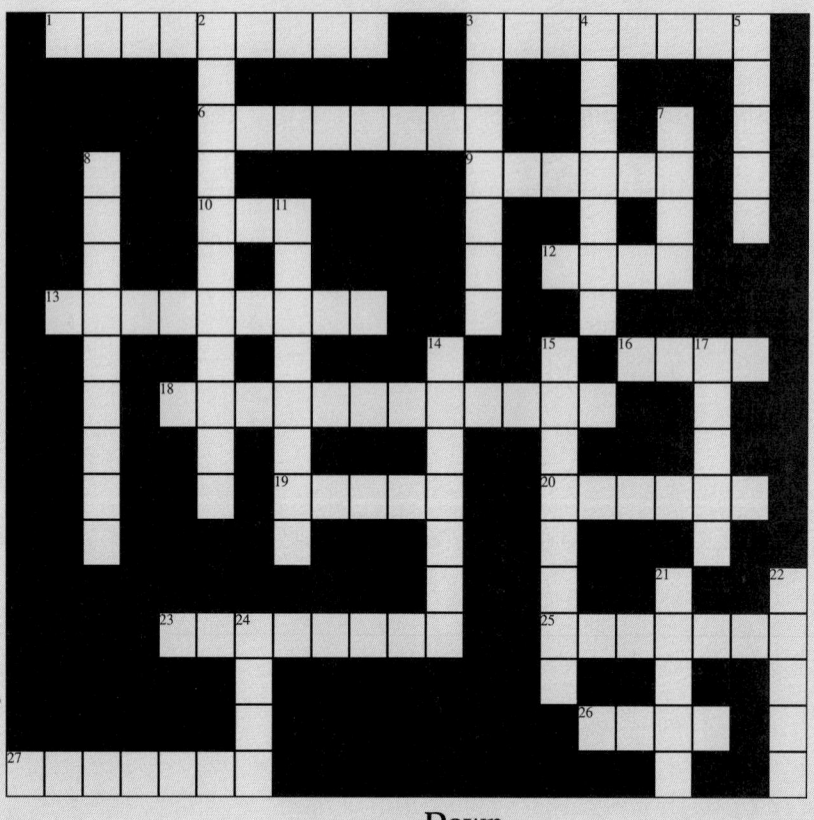

Across

1. Monks live in a _____.
3. Saint _____ was a pioneer in founding monasteries.
6. Teachers of false doctrines are called _____.
9. Constantine's mother was _____.
10. Bishops were sometimes called on to maintain _____ and order.
12. Vandals destroyed and looted _____.
13. After Paul, the Church was probably most influenced by _____.
16. The empire in the _____ collapsed by 700 C.E.
18. In time, monasteries became centers of _____.
19. Pope Gregory the _____ brought order to the Church.
20. Muhammad and the Islam religion united the tribes of _____.
23. The feudal system was organized around small _____.
25. Saint Patrick was a missionary in _____.
26. Saint Benedict's motto was "_____ and work."
27. _____ lived alone in the desert, in prayer and fasting.

Down

2. Saint _____ was Saint Benedict's sister.
3. An ecumenical council is a gathering of _____ from around the world.
4. Persecution ended when Constantine became _____.
5. Monks started schools to _____ people to read and write.
7. Sometimes a hermit would live in a _____.
8. The first council was held in _____.
11. Augustine is known for his _____ in theology.
14. Monks and nuns were sometimes called bloodless _____.
15. The _____ movement started with communities of hermits.
17. The Muslims conquered _____ in Europe.
21. The Muslim name for God is _____.
22. The _____ of Milan was issued in 313 C.E.
24. Religious women living in monasteries are called _____.

THE MIDDLE AGES: THE WHEAT AND THE WEEDS—800–1400 C.E.

The wheat and weeds of life

> [Jesus] put before them another parable: "The kingdom of heaven may be compared to someone who sowed good seed in his field; but while everybody was asleep, an enemy came and sowed weeds among the wheat, and then went away. So when the plants came up and bore grain, then the weeds appeared as well. And the slaves of the householder came and said to him, 'Master, did you not sow good seed in your field? Where, then, did these weeds come from?' He answered, 'An enemy has done this.' The slaves said to him, 'Then do you want us to go and gather them?' But he replied, 'No; for in gathering the weeds you would uproot the wheat along with them. Let both of them grow together until the harvest; and at harvest time I will tell the reapers, Collect the weeds first and bind them into bundles to be burned, but gather the wheat into my barn.'"
>
> —Matthew 13:24–30

We have all experienced good and bad times during our lives. Think back over your life and list some of the good memories and moments in the **Wheat** column. Then list some experiences that were difficult or painful for you in the **Weeds** column.

Wheat   **Weeds**

51

An age of contradictions

For our Church, the Middle Ages (800–1400 C.E.) was much like a field filled with wheat and weeds. The people had great faith, but sometimes superstitions and ignorance were mixed in with the faith. Great cathedrals were built. At the same time, armies went about destroying everything in sight. Some popes were holy saints and great leaders. Other popes were weak and pursued worldly ambitions. Monasticism reached its peak, producing great saints, scholars, and leaders. Unfortunately, it also suffered from corruption and worldliness. New religious orders arose that preached peace and brotherly love. It was also during this era that the Crusades took place. This Golden Age of Faith saw a great split in our Church. Truly the good seeds of the gospel and the weeds of evil grew side-by-side during the Middle Ages.

THE COMMUNITY'S INTERACTION WITH SOCIETY AND GOVERNMENT

Charlemagne—the first Holy Roman emperor

This period of history opens under the rule of Charlemagne (Charles the Great). In 800 C.E., Charlemagne led his army to Italy to rescue the pope from Germanic kings who were trying to take over Rome. In the process, he conquered other kings and gained some control over Germany, Italy, and France.

To thank Charlemagne, Pope Leo III crowned him emperor of the Holy Roman Empire on Christmas Day in 800 C.E. Charlemagne's goal was to bring peace and unity back to the empire, so he made many changes during his reign in hopes of achieving his goal of peace. After winning a battle, Charlemagne insisted that the conquered people convert to Christianity. He also declared that Latin be the official language used at all Masses. (This does not change until the Second Vatican Council in the twentieth century.) And Charlemagne's own love for learning motivated him to establish universities and to inspire a growth in architecture. All this was done to fulfill Charlemagne's dream of a new, powerful, and orderly Christian empire.

Yet, this time of "wheat" also had its "weeds." Feudalism still existed, and the kings and princes of the territories were not very willing to surrender their rule to the Holy Roman emperor. Also, many of the

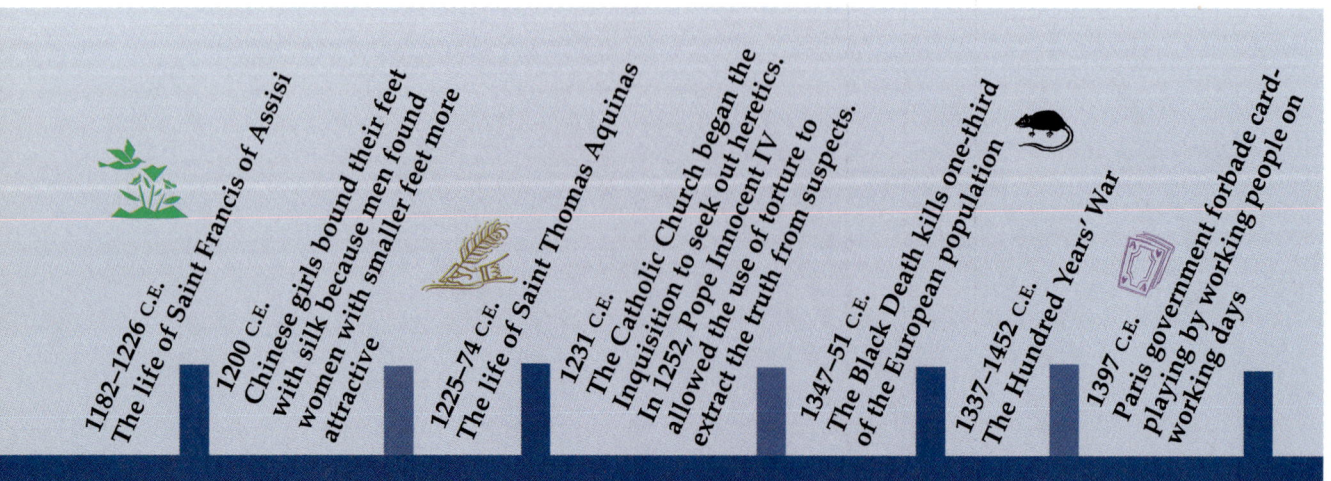

1182–1226 C.E. The life of Saint Francis of Assisi

1200 C.E. Chinese girls bound their feet with silk because men found women with smaller feet more attractive

1225–74 C.E. The life of Saint Thomas Aquinas

1231 C.E. The Catholic Church began the Inquisition to seek out heretics. In 1252, Pope Innocent IV allowed the use of torture to extract the truth from suspects.

1347–51 C.E. The Black Death kills one-third of the European population

1337–1452 C.E. The Hundred Years' War

1397 C.E. Paris government forbade card-playing by working people on working days

recent converts to Christianity continued to believe in superstitions because they received very little education in their new faith.

Therefore the dream of one united Catholic Europe with one faith and one emperor did not become a reality.

TRIVIA TEASER

Charlemagne, the first Holy Roman emperor, was six feet four inches tall. This was considered quite tall, since the average height of men during this period was about five feet four inches.

Dialogue Corner

In a group of four, develop a plan to create a peaceful empire in your school, parish, or neighborhood. Your strategy should consist of three steps that need to be completed to achieve your goal. After all the groups have finished, compare plans. Then, together as a class, discuss and develop a final plan using some of the steps the groups have developed.

Who's in charge?

From that Christmas Day when Pope Leo III crowned Charlemagne emperor, a political question began to trouble the Church. Who is more powerful—the pope who represents Jesus or the emperor who has the legal power to rule society (and also has armies to support him)?

The issue was never really settled. At times the emperor and monarchy would obey the pope. At other times, the ruling government would ignore the pope and disregard the laws of the Church. They would rule how they wanted to rule, not how the Church wanted society ruled. Or the rulers would force or trick the pope to support their political rule.

This struggle for power often confused the faithful who were caught in the middle. Should they support the pope and disobey the emperor? That could mean trouble, since the emperor had armies to support him and his laws. Or should they disobey the pope and support the emperor? Would the betrayal of their faith and their conscience make God angry? This power struggle between the popes and emperors or monarchies was a major problem for our ancestors in faith throughout this period in history.

"No slave can serve two masters; for a slave will either hate the one and love the other, or be devoted to the one and despise the other. You cannot serve God and wealth."

—Luke 16:13

Think of a time in your life when you had to make a decision between doing something for the good of the community (serving God) and doing something that would gain you a personal reward (serving yourself). Write a short explanation about what you chose to do and why.

Peace and politics?

A new wave of invasions occurred during the period from 850 to 1150 C.E. The Vikings came down from the North to raid cities in France and England, while the Muslims invaded Europe from the South, and the Slavic tribes invaded from the East. Churches and monasteries, rich in sacred treasures, were a favorite target of the invaders. Wherever they attacked, a path of death and destruction was left behind. Meanwhile, more battles were being fought internally between small feudal kingdoms in hopes of acquiring new lands.

This age—famous for its knights and chivalry—considered fighting the noble and honorable way to solve differences. Civilization seemed to revolve around war. And when there was no war going on, the kings and their knights held mock wars in the form of tournaments.

Of course, all this fighting had the most effect on the peasants. Their farmlands were trampled by the local armies. And what was left of their crops was taken by the government. To staff the armies, the sons of the peasants were forced to join. And what little money the peasants were able to make went to taxes to pay for war expenses.

In the midst of all the fighting, many popes and bishops tried to promote peace every way they could. For example, the Church passed a law that made it a sin to fight on Sundays. Eventually, it was against Church law to fight on Thursday, Friday, and Saturday as well. Sometimes Church laws were able to stop the fighting, but most of the time they did not have much influence. Even worse, at times some bishops and popes formed armies of their own and joined in the fighting.

Wars plagued society and the Church during the Middle Ages. Still, the rulers and the people of these countries considered themselves Christians, followers of Jesus, our Prince of Peace! During these years many Christians strove to keep the wheat of faith alive among the weeds of war.

What's your view?

What are other ways of resolving conflicts aside from fighting? How do you resolve your differences when you've had an argument with a friend? With a parent? How do you feel if you don't resolve a conflict with someone you care about?

TRIVIA TEASER

Castles during this period were usually cold, smoky, uncomfortable places to live. There was no central heating or plumbing, and the moat surrounding the castle was usually filled with garbage and smelled terrible. Most North American people today live more luxuriously and comfortably than many kings, queens, and nobles of the past.

THE COMMUNITY'S SPIRITUAL LIFE

Simple faith

Although there was a lot of fighting during this period of history, it was a Golden Age of Faith. In actuality, the majority of the people lived lives of sincere faith despite the way many of their rulers acted. Even some of the rulers themselves were people of great faith, such as King Louis of France, who became a canonized saint.

Our ancestors lived a life of simple faith during this period. Remember, most were peasants, uneducated and unable to read or write. They worked many hard hours, but yet they lived in poverty. Often these people suffered from violence and injustice at the hands of the rulers. Yet they found hope in Jesus and the gospel.

For most people, life centered on the Church. They looked to it to teach them the gospel, for protection against unjust rulers, and for salvation. In addition, the Church added fun and enjoyment to their lives through celebrations of great feast days and holy days. Every Sunday was a day of rest, as were most of the major feast days. On many of these feast days, Mass was followed by great festivals. There were carnivals, plays, dancing, and feasting. The more important the feast day, the bigger the celebration. Fortunately for everyone, the Church celebrated many holy days each year during the Middle Ages.

Even the church buildings themselves, which the people helped build, were a source of joy for the faithful. Most peasants lived in poor, dismal conditions. But in their local church or monastery they could see great works of art and hear beautiful music. The liturgies were full of mystery, beauty, and drama. The processions were magnificent; the bishop and the clergy wore dazzling vestments decorated in gold and jewels. In those days, going to Mass was often the high point of the week for many people.

TRIVIA TEASER

Bibles were very scarce and valuable during the Middle Ages. The Bibles kept in the churches were chained to their stands to keep thieves from stealing them.

Dialogue Corner

In our fast-paced society today, Sunday is rarely set aside as a day of total rest. Share your opinion with the class about the benefits of all Christians in the world keeping Sunday as a day of rest.

Catechism Connection

The Church is in history, but at the same time she transcends it. It is only "with the eyes of faith" [*Roman Catechism* I, 10, 20.] that one can see her in her visible reality and at the same time in her spiritual reality as bearer of divine life. (770)

Age of Devotions

Today some of what we learn about historical events may be a combination of fact and fiction. Legends and stories get mixed in with historical facts, perhaps to make the event more interesting and exciting. This same mixing of fact and fiction occurred during the Middle Ages regarding the lives of the saints. Stories of the deeds and miracles of the saints grew, often into fantastic tales. In each community, special devotions arose around certain saints. Statues, shrines, and medals in honor of these saints became very popular.

As is typical, superstitions got mixed with faith. People prayed to their favorite saints for everything from protection against devils to curing a sick cow. The use of sacramentals such as medals and holy water got mixed with good luck charms, such as a rabbit's foot or a deer's horn. Together with these superstitions, though, was a sincere trust in God's love and God's power to save.

Many of our most popular and beautiful devotions began during this same period. The rosary, the stations of the cross, the Christmas crib, medals, scapulars, and devotions to the Blessed Sacrament all began during this period in our Church's history.

It was also during this time that many of the great cathedrals of Europe were built as monuments of faith to honor Jesus, the Son of God, and his mother Mary. Sometimes it took several hundred years to complete the project. All stonework, every wood carving, and the stained-glass windows that decorated the cathedrals were seen as works of love and faith, carried out by the community of disciples of Jesus. Building a cathedral was truly a community effort; everyone helped in one way or another. This community effort is an excellent example of the depth and sincerity of the faith of people at this time. By looking at these cathedrals, we can learn a lot from our "uneducated" ancestors about true faith and what their simple faith produced.

Good luck!

List three areas in life where some people rely on "good luck" to help get them through.

1.

2.

3.

Why is having faith in God better than the greatest "good luck" there is?

Do you believe in "good luck" charms? If so, what are some specific ones that you have used?

_____
_____

TRIVIA TEASER

While building a cathedral during this period, the people in one particular city formed a line almost fifty miles long so they could pass stones to one another from a quarry to the building site.

THE COMMUNITY'S UNDERSTANDING OF THE GOSPEL MESSAGE

Age of Scholars

Some of our Church's greatest theologians and philosophers lived during this age. Therefore, this period is often referred to as the Age of Scholars. Many of the great universities of Europe were founded during this period, and—as you would expect in an age of faith—theology and philosophy were the main courses of study.

For the most part, the scholars during this period were monks, clergy, and the sons of nobles. Thanks to the work of the earlier monks who had copied and preserved ancient manuscripts, the scholars during the Middle Ages were able to study the writings of such great philosophers as Plato and Aristotle.

Have you met . . . *Saint Thomas Aquinas (1225–74)*

It is hard to single out one great scholar and theologian of this time because there were so many. But Saint Thomas Aquinas (1225–74) is perhaps the best known. He is undoubtedly one of the greatest minds to have ever lived.

Saint Thomas was born of a noble family near Aquino, Italy. He began his studies at the age of five at Monte Cassino, the famous monastery founded by Saint Benedict in the fifth century. As a young man, Saint Thomas joined the Dominican Order. He followed the Rule of Saint Dominic and took the religious vows of poverty, celibacy, and obedience. Saint Thomas was as devoted to prayer as he was to study.

As a youth, Thomas was quiet and shy. He did not give the appearance of being exceptionally intelligent but grew up to write one of the greatest explanations of our faith the world has ever seen. The explanations and insights of *Summa Theologica* (a complete summary of all theology) have shaped our understanding of the gospel ever since.

Saint Thomas Aquinas' ideas and explanations were so new and advanced for this period that some Church officials and theologians refused to accept them. They were afraid he was corrupting the faith, especially since he often drew on Roman and Greek philosophers to help explain the mysteries of the Church.

Saint Thomas had such a great power of concentration that he was able to dictate on four different topics to four different secretaries at the same time. While one was writing down what he said on one subject, he would switch to another subject and dictate the next thought on that topic. Keep in mind, Saint Thomas was not dictating letters. He was dictating profound ideas in philosophy and theology. Now that is an exceptional scholar!

Three things are necessary for salvation: to know what we ought to believe; to know what we ought to desire; and to know what we ought to do.

—Saint Thomas Aquinas

SPECIAL PEOPLE, SPECIAL SKILLS

List three people you feel have been blessed with a special skill and what that skill is.

1.

2.

3.

God has blessed each one of us with special gifts to share with the community. One of the special gifts that I have been given is: _____
_____

THE COMMUNITY'S MISSION

The Bible or the sword?

Most of the tribes who had surrounded the Roman Empire were converted to Christianity by the beginning of the Middle Ages. One exception was the Slavic tribes who lived in northeastern Europe. Two brothers, Saints Cyril and Methodius, are credited with bringing the gospel to these people in the ninth century. Once converted, the Slavic peoples maintained a strong faith and helped defend Christianity against Muslim invasions.

During this time, the Muslims were driven out of most of Europe but continued to control the East, including the Holy Land. In the lands they did control, civilization flourished. Great advancements were made in philosophy, art, architecture, literature, and the sciences, such as astronomy and math.

In the tenth century, Turkish tribes waged war on the Arab Muslims. As the Turks successfully conquered the Muslims, they converted to the religion of Islam. Filled with success and vigor, the Turkish converts began to battle Christian countries in the East. In the past, Arab Muslims had allowed pilgrimages to the Holy Land, but the Turks began to kill and persecute Christians who made the journey. Something had to be done. It was then that the Church decided to supplement the Bible with the sword.

The Crusades

Because war was a part of life during this time, many Christians were accustomed to fighting. They decided it was time to stop killing each other and join forces to battle the Turkish non-believers. From this, the idea of a Crusade developed. (*Crusade* comes from the Latin word *crux,* meaning "cross.") Pope Urban II called for the first Crusade in 1095 C.E. Warring Christian kings stopped fighting each other and united to lead a great army to conquer the Muslims and recapture the Holy Land.

The first Crusade was rather successful. The Crusaders drove the Turks from the Holy Land and set up a Christian state there. But old habits die hard. It was not long before the Christian kings were fighting each other again. Eventually, the Turks took advantage of the sparring and regained control of the Holy Land.

Five more Crusades followed between the years 1100 and 1250 C.E. Some Crusades met with success, but most failed for various reasons. Although the idea was noble for that time, killing people to defend a gospel that preaches peace seems contradictory today. And the fact is, faith was not always the motive that sent many people on the Crusades. Knights and others often went looking for money and adventure. They sometimes raped and robbed fellow Christians on their journey to fight the Turks. Indeed, an important factor in the later split between the Church in the East and the Church in the West was the sacking of a major cathedral in the East by the crusaders.

Although they often met their goal, the Crusades are not a positive segment of our Church story. The gospel does not teach us to use swords and fighting to achieve a peaceful end. Thus the Crusades are indeed another example of weeds growing among the wheat.

Dialogue Corner

Although the Crusades in the history of the Church involved violence, it is possible to gather people together and peacefully crusade for a cause. In a small group, come up with an idea for a peaceful crusade that could take place in our world today. Then think of creative ways to carry out your plan. Finally, give your crusade a clever title, such as "Going for Goodness."

- Crusade for: _____
- Peaceful plan of action: _____
  _____
  _____
  _____
- Title: _____

When you have your crusade completely planned, create a poster that advertises your crusade and entices people to join your group.

THE COMMUNITY'S ORGANIZATION

Monks and friars

Around 900 C.E., a great reform began in monastic life, centered around one monastery—Cluny. The reform succeeded for a time in restoring to monastic life the original ideals and virtues of Saint Benedict. Prayer, liturgy, works of charity, schools, and hospitals flourished in these reformed monasteries. By 1000 C.E. there were over 2,000 such monasteries in Europe.

But by the end of this period, many monasteries grew lax again. In reaction to this, the Holy Spirit called two new religious orders into existence. Unlike the Benedictines who lived in monasteries, owned lands, and had peasants to work for them, these two new orders were mendicant, or "beggar," orders. The first, the Franciscan Order, was founded by Saint Francis of Assisi. The second was the Order of Friars Preachers, or the Dominican Order, founded by Saint Dominic.

The Franciscans did not live in monasteries or own property. Instead, they tried to live exactly as Jesus did, depending on God and the charity of others for their daily needs. They devoted themselves to preaching the gospel to the poor. The Dominicans lived much the same as the Franciscans. But they also devoted themselves to learning and to fighting against the heresies that were common in their time. Remember, Saint Thomas Aquinas joined the Dominican Order.

The common people loved these holy, wandering teachers and preachers. The people living in poverty could relate to the Franciscans and the Dominicans because their members did not have much money, either. They lived the gospel in all its purity. And the members of the orders lived right in the midst of the people, not off in some comfortable monastery. They worked at low-paying jobs or begged for their livelihood. Their numbers grew rapidly and so did their influence. The two orders preserved and restored the gospel faith among the people in this time much as Saint Benedict's monks had first done in the fifth and sixth centuries. As you can see, the Spirit always takes care of the Church, raising up new saints in each age.

TRIVIA TEASER

French monks invented the popular game dominoes. The full name is actually *Dixit Dominus Domino Meo*, a Latin phrase in one of the psalms that means "the Lord said to my Lord."

Scripture Search

Read Jesus' parable of the sower in Matthew 13:1–23. As the seed of the gospel is being spread today, describe current examples of each of the places where it lands. For example, where is the gospel message not presently well received—among thorns and weeds?

1. On the edge of the path

2. On rocky ground

3. Among thorns/weeds

4. On good ground

A variety of popes

If the new monastic orders were the pride of this age, the papacy during this time was more of a mixed bag. It had some truly holy and heroic popes such as Leo IX, Pope Saint Gregory VII, Urban II, and Innocent III. These popes loved the Church and protected it from false teachings that could have harmed the community. They led reforms in the monasteries. These leaders were also skilled politicians, able to defend the rights of the Church against ambitious emperors, kings, and nobles.

Other popes weren't quite so skilled or effective. Emperors were able to control them for their political purposes. At one time, a French king forced the pope to go to France so that he could "keep an eye on him." Therefore, the papal government was relocated to Avignon in southern France. A series of French popes at Avignon followed. For the most part, these leaders squeezed money out of the Church to support a luxurious papal palace and an enormous political system. This period, called the *Babylonian Captivity*, lasted from 1309 to 1377 C.E.

In the meantime, a holy and courageous woman named Catherine of Siena became upset because the pope was not in Rome, the traditional place of universal leadership. Catherine visited Pope Gregory XI in Avignon and strongly urged him to return to Rome. He eventually did, and Rome again became the home of the papal government. Because of Saint Catherine's learning and holiness, she was officially declared a reliable teacher and doctor of the Church by Pope Paul VI in 1970.

Meanwhile the German and English rulers elected their own pope. So for much of this time, there seemed to be two popes serving the faith community. And at one point, there were even three men calling themselves the pope of the Christian Church.

Things were not straightened out until 1417 C.E., when one pope ruled over the Church again. But much damage had already been done. People were very confused and had lost confidence in the papacy. Emperors and kings no longer felt much need to pay attention to the papal government. Thus the stage was set for a major revolt among the faithful that, along with theological differences, would eventually split the Church in the next century.

Eastern Christians rejected the rule of the pope in 1054 C.E. This event is called the *Great Schism* (split). The split was based partly on theological reasons and partly on political reasons. Over the next centuries, there were various attempts at reunion, but none lasted very long. So to this day we have two large Christian Churches in the world: the Roman Catholic Church and the Eastern Orthodox Church. In most areas of faith, both Churches are almost identical. The main difference between the Churches revolves around the papacy; the Eastern Orthodox Church does not accept the primary rule of the pope as the Roman Catholics do.

 Scripture Search

Read Matthew 18:5–7. Name some potential scandals that threaten the Church today and then discuss in your group how best to deal with them.

Potential Scandal   **Possible Solution**

Dialogue Corner

In a group of three, talk about people who stood up for something they firmly believed in, hoping that their position would make a difference and force a change.

Have you met . . . *Saint Francis of Assisi (1181–1226)*

Saint Francis of Assisi is an example of faith at its best during the Middle Ages. He felt called to help bring about much needed reform in the Church during this period. Although he was baptized with the name *John*, his friends nicknamed him *Francesco*, and the name stuck.

His father was a wealthy cloth merchant. During his youth, Saint Francis had the reputation of being very social and enjoying the good life. One day while resting near his home at a run-down, tiny chapel named Saint Damien, he had a religious experience. He heard a voice that said, "Repair my house which you see is falling down." At first Saint Francis took this call literally. He used his money to repair the chapel. Later he realized the "house" he was called to repair was the organized Church as a whole.

After a fight with his father over this issue, Saint Francis rejected his inheritance, gave away all his possessions, and spent three years traveling alone as a pilgrim, identifying with the poor and the beggars of his day. Eventually seven disciples joined him, and they formed a little preaching community. Saint Francis, especially, had a genuine gift for preaching. Their message was clear: Return to the simple gospel values and to a love for the crucified Jesus. Their popularity grew gradually.

More men joined his group and Saint Francis formed a Rule to guide them. The Rule stressed loyalty to the Church and a life of strict poverty, which was unlike life in many monasteries at the time. Their houses were to be simple, with no furniture. They often begged for their daily food, which they shared with the poor.

Saint Francis now felt a call to travel as a missionary. His goal was not a simple one—to convert the Muslim Turks to Christianity. After a difficult beginning, he eventually reached the Holy Land and managed to see the Sultan himself. The Sultan was impressed by Saint Francis' holiness but did not embrace the faith.

Saint Francis returned to Italy to find that his little community had grown and was suffering from internal divisions. He never wanted his friars to become priests and didn't want them to become learned theologians. (Saint Francis himself never became a priest, though he was ordained a deacon.) Some of his friars agreed with him, but others did not. Saint Francis then realized it was time for him to resign his leadership and turn it over to others more gifted with skills for directing a large community.

Free of leadership responsibilities, Saint Francis devoted all his time to preaching and prayer. It was at this time that he set up the first Christmas crib. He used simple, concrete methods to help the uneducated understand the basic message of the gospel. Despite his reputation as a romantic and a poet, Saint Francis was actually very strict with himself and had a deep devotion to Jesus.

As stern as Saint Francis was with himself, he was full of love and gentleness toward all people, especially those living in poverty and oppression. His love extended to all of God's creatures, seeing all things as his "brothers and sisters." His peace prayer ("Lord, make me an instrument of your peace . . ."), which is now a popular hymn, is a good example of Saint Francis' approach to life.

His love for nature and his dedication to peace make him a saint for all times, especially with the destruction of the environment and the technology of war we suffer from presently. Saint Francis' community became a major force for "repairing" the Church in the Middle Ages. It continues to be a major force for good to this very day. For these reasons, Saint Francis, the merchant's son from Assisi, has become "everyone's saint."

 One characteristic of Saint Francis of Assisi that I admire most is:
_____
_____
_____

"Rejoice in the Lord always; again I will say, Rejoice. Let your gentleness be known to everyone. The Lord is near. Do not worry about anything, but in everything by prayer and supplication with thanksgiving let your requests be made known to God. And the peace of God, which surpasses all understanding, will guard your hearts and your minds in Christ Jesus" (Philippians 4:4–7).

Briefly discuss ways that young people can make the world a more peaceful place to live. How should we go about promoting peace?

 One area of my life in which I need to pray for more peace is:
_____
_____

Pause to Pray

Together, pray the Prayer of Saint Francis.

*Lord, make me an instrument of your peace;
where there is hatred, let me sow love;
where there is injury, pardon;
where there is doubt, faith;
where there is despair, hope;
where there is darkness, light;
and where there is sadness, joy.
Grant that I may not so much seek to be consoled as to console;
to be understood, as to understand,
to be loved as to love;
for it is in giving that we receive,
it is in pardoning that we are pardoned,
and it is in dying that we are born to eternal life.*

HOMEWORK

Choose one symbol, such as the wheat and the weeds growing together, that you feel best describes the events of the Middle Ages. In the space below, or on a separate piece of paper, draw your symbol. Then label parts of it with appropriate events from this time period.

REBIRTH, REBELLION, AND REFORM—1400–1700 C.E.

Then and now

Listed below are a few of the famed people who lived during this age and what they are famous for. Each person had a profound effect on this time period, an effect that we still witness today. In a group of three, try to name people from the nineteenth and twentieth centuries who have had a similar impact on the world because of their work. Make sure to mention what each person has contributed to society.

Then

Columbus—explorer

Shakespeare—playwright, poet

Saint Teresa of Avila—religious leader and writer

Galileo—astronomer

Michelangelo—artist

Gutenberg—inventor of printing press

Now

1431 C.E. Joan of Arc was burned at the stake in Rouen, France, after being accused of being a witch; she was 19 years old

1492 C.E. Columbus reached the New World

1517 C.E. Martin Luther posted his *Ninety-Five Theses* on the door of Castle Church in Wittenberg

1527 C.E. King Henry VIII of England divorced his wife, Catherine of Aragón—first step in establishing the Anglican Church

1543 C.E. Nicholaus Copernicus published a book detailing his theory that the earth travels around the sun

A time of rebirth

The Renaissance dominated a majority of this period from 1350–1600 C.E. (*Renaissance* is a French word meaning "rebirth.") People of this time looked to the past to reexperience all the wonders of the ancient world—the glory of the great wisdom, art, and architecture of past days in Greece and Rome. During this time of rebirth, there were also great discoveries. A whole new world on the other side of the earth was proven to exist by Columbus and Magellan. In a matter of a few years, the world our ancestors had known suddenly became ten times bigger.

All this discovery, of an ancient world and of a new world, focused the attention of the people on the exciting possibilities and pleasures of the present life. Interest in God and in eternity, so much a part of people's lives during the Middle Ages, suddenly seemed less important.

This new focus led to a lessening of faith in many people, including some who were supposed to be an example of holiness to others—popes, bishops, priests, monks, and nuns. The people soon protested and rebelled against the Church, demanding reform. It did not take long before the Christian Church split into three groups—Catholic, Orthodox, and Protestant.

Recognizing the need for change, the Catholic Church did reform itself. And since that time, the Church has never seen such lax faith or harmful abuses as it did in the first part of this period.

1545–63 C.E. Three Church meetings held at Trent

1607 C.E. Jamestown, Virginia, the first colony in America, established

1620 C.E. The Pilgrims arrived at Plymouth, Massachusetts

1633 C.E. Galileo sentenced to life imprisonment (later, house arrest) for supporting the Copernican theory, which was considered heretical by the Church

THE COMMUNITY'S INTERACTION WITH SOCIETY AND GOVERNMENT

A society of intellectuals and artisans

The following are just a few of the great people who lived and worked during the Renaissance period. See if you can match each person with his or her accomplishment.

_____ 1. Teresa of Avila
_____ 2. Francis Bacon
_____ 3. Columbus
_____ 4. Cortez
_____ 5. Leonardo da Vinci
_____ 6. Vincent de Paul
_____ 7. Erasmus
_____ 8. Galileo
_____ 9. Ignatius of Loyola
_____ 10. Machiavelli
_____ 11. Magellan
_____ 12. Michelangelo
_____ 13. Thomas More
_____ 14. Pizzaro
_____ 15. Queen Elizabeth I
_____ 16. Rembrandt
_____ 17. Shakespeare
_____ 18. Francis Xavier

A. Italian sculptor, painter
B. Florentine painter, sculptor, architect, engineer
C. ruler of England
D. reformed the Carmelite monastic order
E. space scientist, astronomer
F. playwright, poet
G. English statesman and author
H. Dutch scholar
I. Italian statesman and political philosopher
J. English philosopher
K. Italian navigator, reached the New World
L. Portuguese explorer
M. founder of the Society of Jesus
N. French priest, special patron of missionaries
O. French priest, dedicated to caring for the poor
P. Spanish conqueror of Mexico
Q. Spanish conqueror of Peru
R. Dutch painter

An explosion of the human spirit

It is difficult to get a grasp of the "explosion of the human spirit" that took place during the Renaissance Age. Some of the most exciting, creative, adventuresome, and talented people the world has ever seen lived during this period. The contributions they made to society still have a tremendous impact on us today. And spreading the news of their ideas and accomplishments was made much easier thanks to Johann Gutenberg. He invented the first printing press in the middle 1400s. Society was alive and exciting!

Although faith still dominated people's thoughts and concerns, these years often focused on human accomplishments, knowledge, and creativity. This philosophy came to be known as *humanism*. At times the trend in humanism overlapped with people's faith, especially in the area of the arts. Many of the world's great religious masterpieces were created during the Renaissance, including the Sistine Chapel and Saint Peter's Basilica in Rome. Popes and other leaders in the Church often promoted this kind of art.

At the same time, some of the new discoveries and interests that occurred during this period seemed to go against the teachings of the Church. Therefore the Church often found itself opposing some

TRIVIA TEASER
Puritans did not allow the singing of Christmas carols. They considered it too frivolous and irreverent.

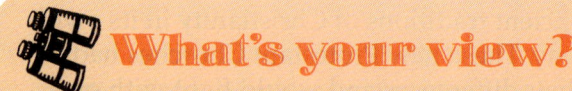
What's your view?
Think of two areas in our world today that suffer from division. Then suggest a possibility for restoring unity.

Protestant roots in the United States

The thirteen original colonies that formed the basis for the United States were, for the most part, founded by immigrants of various Protestant Churches. The Pilgrims, for instance, came to the New World in 1620 for the purpose of having freedom of religion.

As the colonists developed local governments and laws, religion played a major role. Religious leaders often served as civil leaders in the early colonies. Therefore, civil laws quite often reflected Protestant religious or moral beliefs. Nathaniel Hawthorne's famous novel about colonial times, *The Scarlet Letter*, is a good example of this mixture of society and religion. In some colonies, where the strict Puritan form of Protestantism was clearly the religion of the majority, other religions were not tolerated. These colonies were especially suspicious of Catholics. The conflicts between Protestants and Catholics in Europe were not forgotten. However, a few colonies, such as Pennsylvania and Maryland, promoted freedom of all religions. In fact, Maryland was founded primarily as a colony for Catholics.

In general, the ideals of Protestantism, especially the strict Puritan form of Protestantism, played a major role in shaping the life and spirit of our country. These ideals included a strong commitment to independence, personal freedom, and hard work. Activities such as dancing, drinking, and physical pleasures were not encouraged. Education was valued but tended to focus on study of the Bible. Most schools in colonial times, including public schools, taught religion as a required subject.

Catholic missionaries were not very active in the thirteen British colonies. The missionaries worked mostly in the Spanish and French areas of the New World—the central and western parts of North America. These areas did not become part of the United States until the nineteenth century.

It is a real credit to the members of the Continental Congress that they insisted in the Constitution on freedom of religion. Even though Protestants were the majority of the population and held most of the political and economical power, Catholics and other religious minorities received full rights of citizenship and freedom to practice their faith. This willingness to tolerate different faiths helped the United States become a great nation.

THE COMMUNITY'S INTERACTION WITH SOCIETY AND GOVERNMENT

A society of intellectuals and artisans

The following are just a few of the great people who lived and worked during the Renaissance period. See if you can match each person with his or her accomplishment.

_____ 1. Teresa of Avila
_____ 2. Francis Bacon
_____ 3. Columbus
_____ 4. Cortez
_____ 5. Leonardo da Vinci
_____ 6. Vincent de Paul
_____ 7. Erasmus
_____ 8. Galileo
_____ 9. Ignatius of Loyola
_____ 10. Machiavelli
_____ 11. Magellan
_____ 12. Michelangelo
_____ 13. Thomas More
_____ 14. Pizzaro
_____ 15. Queen Elizabeth I
_____ 16. Rembrandt
_____ 17. Shakespeare
_____ 18. Francis Xavier

A. Italian sculptor, painter
B. Florentine painter, sculptor, architect, engineer
C. ruler of England
D. reformed the Carmelite monastic order
E. space scientist, astronomer
F. playwright, poet
G. English statesman and author
H. Dutch scholar
I. Italian statesman and political philosopher
J. English philosopher
K. Italian navigator, reached the New World
L. Portuguese explorer
M. founder of the Society of Jesus
N. French priest, special patron of missionaries
O. French priest, dedicated to caring for the poor
P. Spanish conqueror of Mexico
Q. Spanish conqueror of Peru
R. Dutch painter

An explosion of the human spirit

It is difficult to get a grasp of the "explosion of the human spirit" that took place during the Renaissance Age. Some of the most exciting, creative, adventuresome, and talented people the world has ever seen lived during this period. The contributions they made to society still have a tremendous impact on us today. And spreading the news of their ideas and accomplishments was made much easier thanks to Johann Gutenberg. He invented the first printing press in the middle 1400s. Society was alive and exciting!

Although faith still dominated people's thoughts and concerns, these years often focused on human accomplishments, knowledge, and creativity. This philosophy came to be known as *humanism*. At times the trend in humanism overlapped with people's faith, especially in the area of the arts. Many of the world's great religious masterpieces were created during the Renaissance, including the Sistine Chapel and Saint Peter's Basilica in Rome. Popes and other leaders in the Church often promoted this kind of art.

At the same time, some of the new discoveries and interests that occurred during this period seemed to go against the teachings of the Church. Therefore the Church often found itself opposing some of the new ideas that were springing up everywhere. For instance, the Church did not immediately grasp many of Galileo's astronomical theories and ideas.

The Church's opposition to some new ideas tended to make people feel that the Church was old-fashioned and an obstacle to human growth. These people began to take Church teachings less seriously, putting more of their "faith" in science and in ancient philosophers.

In general, the Church supported and actively promoted much of the new learning, exploration, and art that highlighted this period. Nevertheless, the Church's official leaders and teachings gradually lost the respect and loyalty of many of the faithful. Times were changing, and the people wondered if the Church would ever change.

Dialogue Corner

Discuss the following questions with another student: *If you were an artist, what scene from the Bible or our Church's history would you like to recreate? Why did you choose this particular event?*

TRIVIA TEASER

When Galileo supported the Copernican theory that the earth revolves around the sun, he was challenging the popular belief that sun revolves around the earth. His teaching was considered dangerous to the faith, and he was forced by Church officials to disown his views. However, there is recent evidence that the dispute between Galileo and the Church was really over his views about the Eucharist, which were based on his overall scientific and philosophical views.

Luther's hope of reform

Martin Luther was a brilliant German priest who belonged to the Augustinian Order. He became very upset with the leadership in the Church and with some of the superstitious religious practices that had become common during this time. Luther also believed that the popes and other leaders had strayed from the simple gospel message of Jesus and had become too worldly. He felt they were misleading and oppressing the people.

So Luther decided to protest in hopes of calling the Church back to what he felt was the true message of the gospel. He wrote the *Ninety-Five Theses*, a listing of complaints against the Church, and posted them on the door of Castle Church in Wittenberg on October 31, 1517. Some of his objections dealt with practices of faith, such as excessive devotion to relics of saints. Other objections challenged basic teachings of the Church, such as the nature of the sacraments, including the priesthood.

Pope Leo X told Luther to take back his objections. He refused, so the pope excommunicated him, officially cutting him off from communion with the Church. But Luther's ideals about returning to simple faith and his complaints against the worldliness of Church leaders appealed to Christians living in poverty. In addition, some German nobles, eager to escape paying Church taxes to an Italian pope, defended Luther and helped spread his ideas in their states.

Luther didn't actually plan to start a revolt or a new Church. He wanted simply to help reform the Church he loved and bring it back to the kind of faith he felt the apostles taught. But a religious revolt against the Church and the rule of the pope did begin. And before Luther's death, the Lutheran Church had formed and began spreading throughout Europe.

New Protestant Churches also formed as more concerns were expressed about Christian truths and practices. One of the most popular of these offsprings was Calvinism, which is known today as the Presbyterian Church in the United States and the Reformed Churches in Europe. Each new Church interpreted the gospel and the ancient traditions of Christianity in its own way. These new Protestant Churches had their differences and would fight with one another or within their own Church. But the one thing they all had in common was that they rejected the pope as the successor of Saint Peter and the official representative of Jesus on earth.

TRIVIA TEASER

Martin Luther was the first to put lighted candles on a Christmas tree. They represented the stars that filled the sky on the first Christmas night.

Dialogue Corner

Martin Luther's goal of reformation actually resulted in the beginning of a new Church. Share with a partner about a time in your life when your initial goal regarding a project resulted in something you never intended.

Scripture Search

Read John 10:14–16. If Jesus were to appear to a group of Protestants and Catholics today, what directions and advice do you think he might offer? Write these thoughts in the form of a short speech that Jesus might give.

_____
_____
_____
_____
_____

Compare your speech to what others in your class have written.

Nations take sides

When the Church separated into the Catholic and Protestant religions, individual nations took sides, too. By 1600, Europe was divided into Protestant nations and Catholic nations. England, the Netherlands, Sweden, and the North German States adopted the Protestant religion. Ireland, Spain, France, Italy, Poland, and the South German States followed the Catholic Church. There were frequent wars between the Protestant and Catholic countries. Persecutions even returned, but this time it was Catholics persecuting Protestants and vice versa—Christians persecuting Christians!

It is no surprise that mistrust and dislike between Catholic and Protestant Churches continued over the centuries. The two Churches have actually made progress in attempting to mend their relationship over the past thirty years. They have begun to focus on the aspects of their faith that they share in common as disciples of Jesus as opposed to concentrating on the differences.

Russia chose to follow the Eastern Orthodox Church, formed during the Great Schism in the Middle Ages. And the Arab and Turkish countries surrounding the Mediterranean Sea continued to practice Islam. The dream that dominated the Middle Ages—one Holy Roman Empire ruled by one emperor and guided by one faith—was no longer realistic. In a place where there was once one faith, by 1600 there were basically three different Christian Churches and Islam.

TRIVIA TEASER
Puritans did not allow the singing of Christmas carols. They considered it too frivolous and irreverent.

What's your view?
Think of two areas in our world today that suffer from division. Then suggest a possibility for restoring unity.

Protestant roots in the United States

The thirteen original colonies that formed the basis for the United States were, for the most part, founded by immigrants of various Protestant Churches. The Pilgrims, for instance, came to the New World in 1620 for the purpose of having freedom of religion.

As the colonists developed local governments and laws, religion played a major role. Religious leaders often served as civil leaders in the early colonies. Therefore, civil laws quite often reflected Protestant religious or moral beliefs. Nathaniel Hawthorne's famous novel about colonial times, *The Scarlet Letter*, is a good example of this mixture of society and religion. In some colonies, where the strict Puritan form of Protestantism was clearly the religion of the majority, other religions were not tolerated. These colonies were especially suspicious of Catholics. The conflicts between Protestants and Catholics in Europe were not forgotten. However, a few colonies, such as Pennsylvania and Maryland, promoted freedom of all religions. In fact, Maryland was founded primarily as a colony for Catholics.

In general, the ideals of Protestantism, especially the strict Puritan form of Protestantism, played a major role in shaping the life and spirit of our country. These ideals included a strong commitment to independence, personal freedom, and hard work. Activities such as dancing, drinking, and physical pleasures were not encouraged. Education was valued but tended to focus on study of the Bible. Most schools in colonial times, including public schools, taught religion as a required subject.

Catholic missionaries were not very active in the thirteen British colonies. The missionaries worked mostly in the Spanish and French areas of the New World—the central and western parts of North America. These areas did not become part of the United States until the nineteenth century.

It is a real credit to the members of the Continental Congress that they insisted in the Constitution on freedom of religion. Even though Protestants were the majority of the population and held most of the political and economical power, Catholics and other religious minorities received full rights of citizenship and freedom to practice their faith. This willingness to tolerate different faiths helped the United States become a great nation.

THE COMMUNITY'S SPIRITUAL LIFE

An increase in saints

Throughout the Renaissance, the Holy Spirit delivered new saints to help get the Church back on the right track. Among such saints were Vincent de Paul, Teresa of Avila (Jesus), Francis de Sales, and Thomas More. These people lived exemplary lives of faith.

Saint Vincent de Paul served the people in his day similar to how Mother Teresa served the people of India in the twentieth century. He dedicated himself to caring for the poor and homeless. In the process, he called for a new awareness of and concern for people living in poverty. Saint Vincent de Paul also founded a religious community for men (the Vincentians) and with Saint Louise de Marillac, another for women (the Sisters of Charity). Today, these communities still carry the message and mission of Saint Vincent de Paul.

Saint Teresa of Avila, a Spanish woman with great energy and courage, led a reform of monastic life. She began with her own community, the Carmelite Order. Her dedication to prayer and a life of penance set an example that called the whole Church to a renewal in the Spirit.

Saint Francis de Sales, a French bishop, was a model for all bishops to follow. He was a brilliant teacher of the faith and defended it skillfully against the Protestant challenge. More importantly, he was a man of deep love and prayer. By his preaching, writing, and example, Saint Francis de Sales led his followers—and the Church at large—back to a life of faith and devotion. His most famous book, *The Introduction to the Devout Life*, was written especially for lay people. It is still being used today as a guide to holiness for all people.

Saint Thomas More was a husband, father, humanist scholar, and brilliant statesman. For a time, he was the best friend and closest advisor to King Henry VIII of England. When Henry VIII took the throne, England was Catholic. But Henry encountered difficulty with the Church when he wanted to divorce his wife. The pope, citing Church law, would not allow the divorce. So Henry declared himself head of the Church of England (now the Anglican Church). He forced all residents of England to declare loyalty to him rather than to the pope. If people refused, they were executed as traitors.

Thomas, a devout Catholic, refused to side with Henry. He chose loyalty to Jesus over loyalty to his king. So Henry VIII had Thomas executed as a traitor. Saint Thomas More's brave example gave many other Catholics the courage to remain loyal to the Church. For many years to come, the papists (people loyal to the pope) were persecuted in both England and Ireland.

Dialogue Corner

In a group of four, discuss the following question: *What types of new saints do you think Jesus and his Spirit are calling in our time? List some of your ideas below:*

_____
_____
_____
_____

TRIVIA TEASER

Leonardo da Vinci, appropriately called a "Renaissance man" because of his many talents, sketched out the basic design for airplanes and machine guns during this period. All his writings were written backwards. Therefore, they could only be read in a mirror!

New religious communities

The Spirit didn't call upon only individuals to help bring reform and renewal to the Church. New religious communities also formed. The Vincentians and the Sisters of Charity, founded by Saint Vincent de Paul and Saint Louise de Marillac, were just two of the many communities that formed at this time. But these new communities were different from the earlier monasteries that helped reform the Church.

These new religious communities were modeled most closely after the groups formed by Saint Francis of Assisi and Saint Dominic. The members lived in the middle of town in simple houses called *convents* rather than in large, remote monasteries. Instead of withdrawing from society into the "desert," the religious men and women went directly into the "marketplace" to care for the poor and needy. Thus they combined a monastic life of prayer and penance with practical service in society. Eventually, the communities operated schools, hospitals, and orphanages.

One such community was the Brothers of the Christian Schools, founded by Saint John Baptist de la Salle. (Today the community is simply referred to as the Christian Brothers.) The men who joined this community devoted themselves to operating schools for people who were neglected by society— mostly orphans and those living in poverty.

The Visitation Sisters, founded by Saint Jane de Chantal, was another example of a community devoted to helping people. Saint Jane de Chantal was a French noblewoman, wife, and mother. She was also a good friend of Saint Francis de Sales. After her husband died, Jane decided she wanted to become a nun. Under the guidance of Francis, she formed a new community for women, one of the first communities of sisters to perform services of charity outside monastery walls. At first, this created quite a scandal because people expected nuns to live behind monastery walls. But eventually the idea was accepted, and since that time, many similar communities of sisters have been established.

If you were to establish a religious order today, what services would you choose to perform as part of the mission of the community?
_____
_____
_____

Saint Ignatius and the Society of Jesus

The most famous religious community to form at this time was the Society of Jesus, often referred to as the Jesuit community. A Spanish nobleman and soldier, Ignatius of Loyola had a deep religious experience while recovering from war wounds he suffered in 1521. He felt called to form a group of disciples totally dedicated to the Church and to the pope. They would defend the faith against Protestant errors—not by the sword, but by scholarship and sound teaching.

Ignatius organized his community in a military fashion, demanding "loyal obedience" to its leaders. New members had to undertake a long training period in the spiritual life and in theology before they could begin to teach.

It wasn't long before the Jesuits seemed to be everywhere—teaching, preaching, and advising kings and the pope. They sent missionaries to the far parts of the New World, establishing schools and universities wherever they settled. The order soon became famous for its scholars and for its loyalty to the Church. Many saints arose from the Jesuit community, including Saint Francis Xavier, Saint Isaac Jogues, and Saint Aloysius Gonzaga. Since the beginning, the Jesuits have played a key role in promoting and defending the faith.

Read Saint Ignatius of Loyola's Prayer for Generosity.

Teach us, good Lord, to serve you as you deserve:
To give and not to count the cost;
To fight and not to heed the wounds;
To toil and not to seek for rest;
To labor and not to ask for any reward
Save that of knowing that we do your will.

In a small group, write a prayer that teaches these same values of generosity. Then share your prayer with the rest of the class.

The people in the pew

The Renaissance affected everyone. A "middle class" developed in society between the nobles and the peasants. Members of the middle class lived in towns and cities, usually working as merchants or in skilled trades and crafts. Most importantly, these people had access to education. Because of the invention of the printing press, books were finally available to almost everyone. More and more people learned to read and write.

So when the great debates between Catholics and Protestants began, most of the faithful were able follow along. People were no longer totally dependent upon the clergy and monks to teach them. A new interest in the gospel arose among the people, ending many of the superstitious religious practices. Overall, a more enlightened faith began to develop in the people.

The examples of the saints and the good works being performed by the new religious communities had a great impact on the "people in the pew." The excitement of the humanist movement was matched by a renewal of faith and an overall reform of the Church.

THE COMMUNITY'S UNDERSTANDING OF THE GOSPEL MESSAGE

The Council of Trent

As Protestantism began to spread, Church leaders did what other Church leaders had done since the time of the apostles. They called a special council of all bishops to identify the true teachings of the faith. This council took place at Trent, Italy, in three sessions, spanning nearly twenty years: 1545–47, 1551–52, and 1562–63.

The following were some key ideas of the Protestants that the bishops discussed at the council:

- Ordination, Anointing of the Sick, Confirmation, Penance, and Marriage are not really sacraments.
- The Bible is the only real teaching authority in the Church. Each person is free to interpret the Bible for himself or herself. The pope and bishops have no special teaching authority.
- Jesus is not really present in the Eucharist in the way the Church teaches; the Mass is not really a sacrifice, and devotion to the Blessed Sacrament is wrong.
- Devotion to Mary and the saints, devotion to relics, and the use of sacramentals—statues, holy water, rosaries, medals—are wrong.
- Nothing taught after the first eight Church councils is necessarily true and does not have to be believed.
- It is not necessary to support or respect monks and nuns. They are not following the gospel in the way they lived.

Other topics challenged by the Protestants included the nature of sin, grace, and free will. Protestant theologians gave scholarly arguments for all their ideas. At the time, many wrong things were being taught and practiced by the Church leaders and the people, so there was some truth to their complaints. When the bishops met at Trent, they knew they had their work cut out for them.

Dilemmas and decisions

There were two levels to the work of the Council of Trent. The focus on one level was the theology, or Church teachings. The other level focused on Church practices. Both levels were equally important, and the bishops were very successful in bringing much-needed reform to these two aspects of the Church.

The bishops studied all the major theological issues raised by the Protestants. After reviewing the issues, they carefully redefined numerous official Church teachings and practices. In the process, the bishops cleared up popular errors and superstitions that had invaded the Church over the centuries.

The bishops tackled many difficult issues during the Council of Trent. The following are a few points the council made regarding some of the Protestant teachings.

- The pope and bishops have an official duty to teach in the name of Jesus and for the whole Church. Private interpretation of the Bible is not enough.
- There are seven sacraments; the Mass is a true sacrifice, and Jesus is truly present in the Blessed Sacrament.
- Devotion to Mary and the saints and the use of sacramentals, such as statues, medals, holy water, and relics, are good and should be encouraged.
- The religious life is a valid expression of the gospel ideals.
- Grace, free will, and original sin were defined.

The council clarified and defended all the major teachings of the Church from the time of the apostles onward. This was no small task. In the process, a written catechism was developed that could be used to teach the Church's truths to all believers. This catechism brought uniformity to the faith.

Also, the Council of Trent established new rules for the clergy to follow to prevent former abuses from happening again. The council set up strict requirements to govern the life of monks and nuns, including guidelines for the use of the property they owned. A program was instituted for seminaries training new priests. And strict regulations were established for bishops to follow that made sure they spent their time caring for the community.

Catechism Connection

Christ instituted the sacraments of the new law. There are seven: Baptism, Confirmation (or Chrismation), the Eucharist, Penance, the Anointing of the Sick, Holy Orders and Matrimony. . . . (1210)

Catechism Connection

We must therefore consider the Eucharist as:
• thanksgiving and praise to the *Father*;
• the sacrificial memorial of *Christ* and his Body;
• the presence of Christ by the power of his word and of his *Spirit*. (1358)

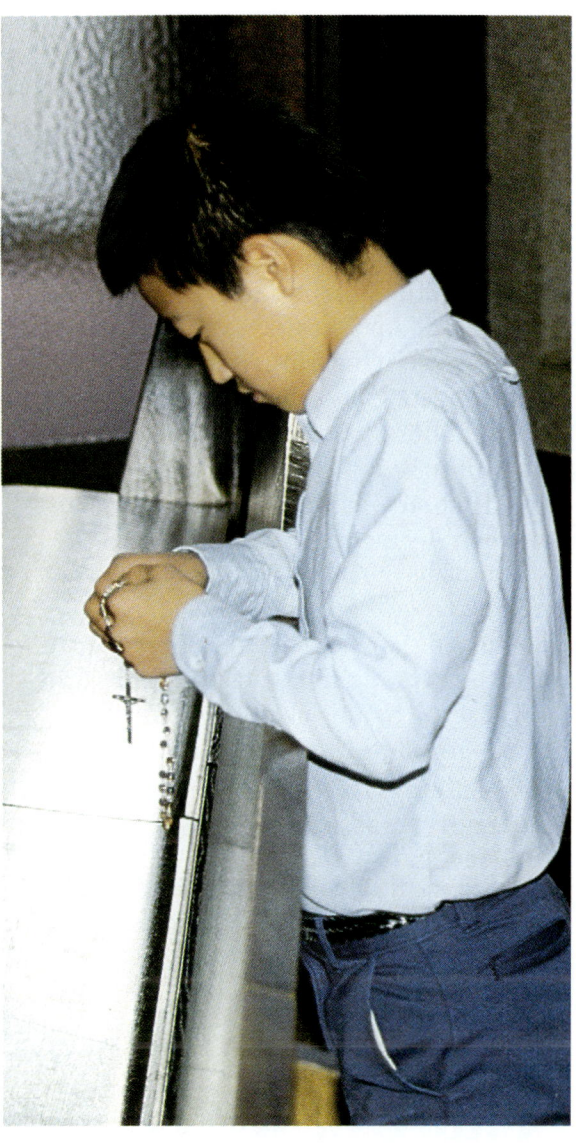

Results of the Council of Trent

The immediate result of the council was to give clarity and direction to the faithful. Any doubts about what the Church taught or questions about how Catholics differed from Protestants in their beliefs were cleared. People knew exactly what to believe and why, resulting in a more unified Church. The pope and Church leaders regained the confidence of many people.

The council also renewed the spiritual life of the Church. Weakened faith and a desire for worldliness were replaced by enthusiasm and devotion to gospel values, such as poverty, prayer, penance, and works of charity.

The Council of Trent set the standards for Catholic teaching and practice for the next four hundred years, until the Second Vatican Council in the 1960s. In a real sense, Jesus and the Spirit saved the Church by means of this council. Although some Protestants did return to the Catholic Church after the Council of Trent, a separation between Protestants and Catholics did remain.

What are some ways you could bring spiritual renewal to your family life?

_____
_____
_____

THE COMMUNITY'S MISSION

Spreading the word

With the discovery of the New World, the Church suddenly found new opportunities for its missionary work. As soon as new land was discovered, missionaries left Europe to take the gospel message to the native people.

Just about every religious and monastic community sent men and women to the distant shores. Franciscan, Dominican, and the newly-formed Jesuit communities were especially active in the missionary work of bringing the gospel to the new lands.

Most missionaries went to the lands to which their home countries had laid claim. So where the Spanish settled, Spanish missionaries followed. During this time, most Spanish missionaries journeyed to what we now call Central and South America, Mexico, and California. French missionaries traveled to Canada and then followed the Mississippi River down to what is now New Orleans. The Portuguese spread the gospel message in Brazil.

Missionaries also found their way to India. Saint Francis Xavier, a Jesuit priest who is now one of the special patrons of missionaries, helped establish the Church in the Far East (China and Japan).

What's your view?

Where are missionaries needed in the United States today? What is the message that needs to be preached and to whom should they tell it?

TRIVIA TEASER

Brazil, the largest country in South America, was claimed by the Portuguese in 1500. Today, the official language of Brazil is Portuguese, while the other countries in South America speak Spanish.

Culture or the cross

The missionaries during this period were faith-filled and dedicated to bringing the gospel to the people of these new lands. Most lived in great hardship, especially during early missionary work. Some—such as Saint Isaac Jogues, who was tomahawked to death by a group of Iroquois Indians in 1646—died as martyrs.

Unfortunately, the explorers, the governments that sent them, and the settlers who went out to the new lands did not always have the same honorable motives as the missionaries had. Those claiming the land were often looking for wealth and power rather than for converts to the Church. These people treated the natives cruelly, often using force rather than the gospel to gain control. New governments were established, ignoring native customs, languages, and cultures. In the process, some entire civilizations were destroyed.

So this great age of missionary work was often undermined by European exploration and exploitation of the New World. Even as the missionaries shared the faith and built churches and established schools and hospitals, a new culture and new forms of government were being forced upon the native people.

Because of advances in civilization, faith in the true God and in Jesus, his Son, flourishes today in the western hemisphere. So even as some European conquerors were busy planting seeds of evil, the missionaries did succeed in planting the good seeds of the gospel. Both continued to grow side by side.

Guided by Jesus and the Spirit, the Church of the Renaissance proved once again its ability to survive both internal divisions and the external challenges of society. Throughout history, our Church has shown its ability to adapt, survive, and continue to grow, despite human weaknesses. That is as true today as it was in the past because Jesus has promised to stay with the Church until the end of time.

TRIVIA TEASER

The invention of the printing press just prior to Luther's protest played a major role in helping spread his ideas throughout Europe. It became possible to mass-produce books and pamphlets that at one time were copied by hand.

What's missing?

Did you notice that the last section, "The Community's Organization," is missing in this chapter? That's because the organization of the Church in this period was tied directly to the reforms begun by the Council of Trent. Dominating the scene were the Protestant revolt against Catholicism and the great reform of the Catholic Church. A New World was discovered across the ocean. Society experienced a rebirth in learning, art, and science. At the same time, the Church experienced a rebirth in faith, devotion, and missionary zeal, led by some of our greatest saints and by the work of the new religious communities established during this period.

"Go therefore and make disciples of all nations, baptizing them in the name of the Father and of the Son and of the Holy Spirit, and teaching them to obey everything that I have commanded you. And remember, I am with you always, to the end of the age" (Matthew 28:19–20).

Briefly discuss how people your age can serve as missionaries in the world today.

Explain one time during the past week when you served as a missionary.
_____
_____
_____

PAUSE TO PRAY

Leader: *God, knowing you call all of us to be your disciples and to spread the gospel to others, we pray that you will help us remain strong in our faith and imitate the examples of the missionaries and saints.*

Let us pause to reflect on the words of a prayer written by Saint Thérèse of Lisieux, a Carmelite.

Group one: *Christ has no body now but yours, no hands, no feet on earth but yours.*

Group two: *Yours are the eyes through which he looks for compassion on this world.*

Group one: *Yours are the feet with which he walks to do good.*

Group two: *Yours are the hands with which he blesses all the world.*

All: *Yours are the hands. Yours are the feet. Yours are the eyes. You are his body.*

Group one: *Christ has no body now but yours, no hands, no feet on earth but yours.*

Group two: *Yours are the eyes through which he looks for compassion on this world.*

All: *Christ has no body now on earth but yours.*

HOMEWORK

Just as the Renaissance Church was in need of reform, so are our lives. Think about the following areas of your own life. For each area, write down two ways that you can improve this particular aspect of your life.

Relationships with family
1. _____
2. _____

Friendships
1. _____
2. _____

School/relationships with teachers
1. _____
2. _____

Views about Church and faith
1. _____
2. _____

How you spend your time
1. _____
2. _____

Your attitude
1. _____
2. _____

SACRED, SECULAR, SCIENTIFIC— 1700–1950 C.E.

Inventing for the future

Name ten inventions with which you are familiar. Then list a positive and negative effect of each invention. If possible, use examples of how these inventions have affected our Church and faith.

Invention	Benefit	Downfall
1.		
2.		
3.		
4.		
5.		
6.		
7.		
8.		
9.		
10.		

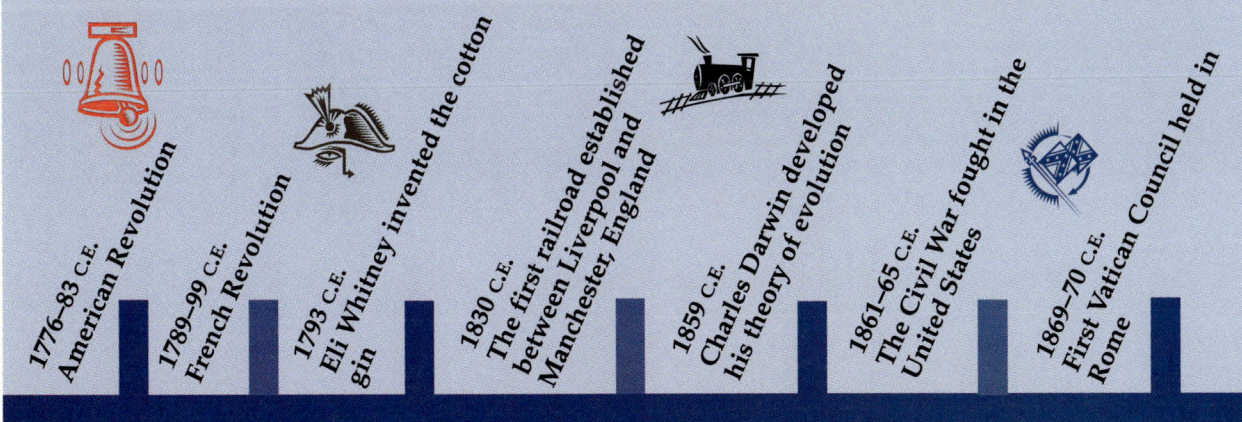

1776–83 C.E. American Revolution
1789–99 C.E. French Revolution
1793 C.E. Eli Whitney invented the cotton gin
1830 C.E. The first railroad established between Liverpool and Manchester, England
1859 C.E. Charles Darwin developed his theory of evolution
1861–65 C.E. The Civil War fought in the United States
1869–70 C.E. First Vatican Council held in Rome

An era of advancement

The events that occurred during the Renaissance played a major role in what happened during the period from 1700–1950 C.E. Society became more independent of the Church. Powerful nations formed, guided by scientific knowledge rather than by faith. We call this new spirit *secularism* (worldliness). The Catholic Church resisted the trend toward secularism during this period.

Many scientific and political revolutions occurred during the nineteenth century. The Industrial Revolution, from 1700 to 1950, was the most influential, replacing human workers with machines. When this period began, people still traveled by horse and lit their home with candles. By the end of this era, 250 years later, people were traveling by jet and watching television in their homes. Given these political and scientific upheavals, the Church that began in the villages and fields of Galilee 1,700 years earlier had some great adjustments to make in a short time. It did, and it emerged at the end of this period stronger and better organized than ever. The test of survival the Church experienced during this time is the story of this chapter.

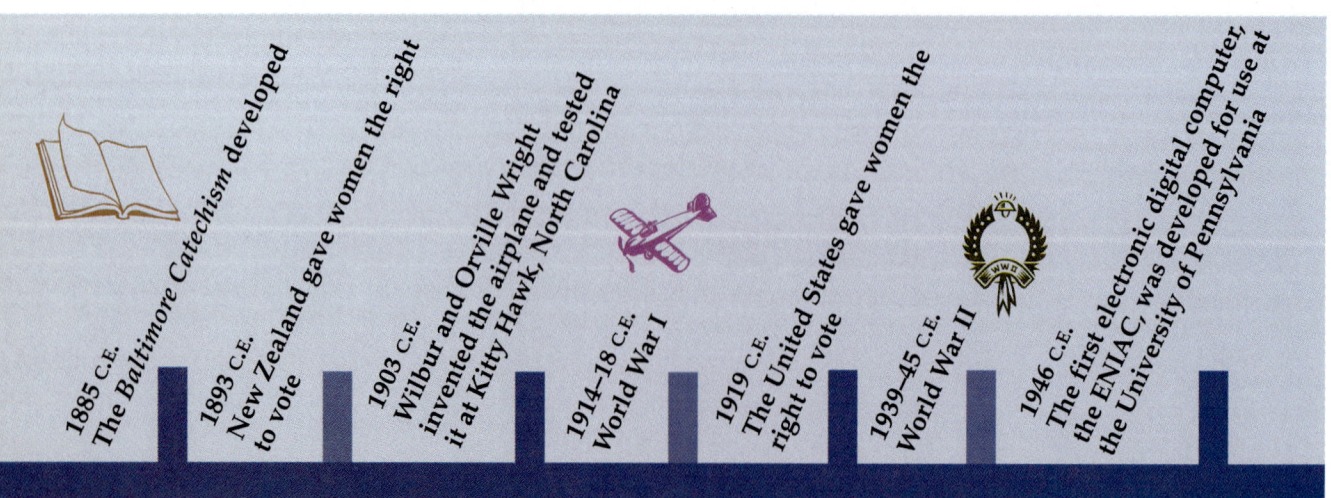

1885 C.E. The Baltimore Catechism developed

1893 C.E. New Zealand gave women the right to vote

1903 C.E. Wilbur and Orville Wright invented the airplane and tested it at Kitty Hawk, North Carolina

1914–18 C.E. World War I

1919 C.E. The United States gave women the right to vote

1939–45 C.E. World War II

1946 C.E. The first electronic digital computer, the ENIAC, was developed for use at the University of Pennsylvania

THE COMMUNITY'S INTERACTION WITH SOCIETY AND GOVERNMENT

Political revolution

Rome and Greece were actually the first societies in recorded history to practice a degree of democracy as their form of government. But around the time of the birth of Jesus, these democracies gave way to rule by an all-powerful emperor, beginning with the reign of Augustus Caesar. When the Roman Empire collapsed, a feudal form of government developed with kings and nobility ruling the small kingdoms. At this time the majority of the people were peasants who had no real rights or say in how they were governed.

Throughout the Middle Ages and the Renaissance, the small kingdoms in Europe gradually developed into a few large nations, including France, Spain, England, Poland, and Russia. But the governments of these nations were still feudal. In each of the nations, an all-powerful king and a group of nobles had all the wealth and control over the people.

This situation began to change in the eighteenth century. The ancient ideals of freedom and democracy were rediscovered. Peasant peoples and a growing middle class grew tired of being bullied and oppressed by the ruling nobility. This dissatisfaction ultimately led to a wave of revolutions in the eighteenth and nineteenth century, including the American Revolution and the French Revolution.

But the past forms of government were not easily forgotten. It wasn't until the twentieth century that democratic forms of government were instituted in many European countries. Even then, countries such as England still held on to the symbols of the old feudal system, such as their king and queen, their lords, and their palaces.

What's your view?

Would you say your family structure is more like a monarchy (one ruler), a democracy (many rulers), or a combination of the two? Discuss your views with the class.

Industrial and scientific revolution

In 1750, people made cloth by hand and traveled on horseback or by carriage—just the way our ancestors had done two thousand years before! In a matter of a few generations, people drastically changed thousands of years of human traditions. They harnessed water power and then steam power. A whole manufacturing system developed with the use of factories, railroads, and steamships, revolutionizing how people manufactured goods and how they transported what was made. To find work, people moved from farms to towns. Soon large cities developed. At the beginning of this period, over 90 percent of the population lived and worked on farms in the United States. Today this statistic has dropped to less than 10 percent.

Modern chemistry, physics, biology, and mathematics got their start during this same period. Important discoveries in all these fields laid the foundations for many "miracles" we experience today, such as organ transplants, nuclear energy, vaccines, skyscrapers, computers, and jet planes.

No one dreamed of such things back in the 1800s. But steam power excited people as much back then as the laser excites us today. People then were also excited about the manufacture of steel, Pasteur's experiments, Darwin's discoveries, the invention of the telegraph, and the introduction of electric power.

WHERE DO YOU LIVE?

List the benefits of living in a rural area and those of living in a city.

Rural   **City**

Where do you think you will choose to live as an adult?

During the Industrial Revolution, it was common for men, women, and children as young as seven or eight to work in factories and mines twelve hours a day, six days a week. Labor unions and child labor laws eventually put an end to those practices.

Darwin developed his theory of evolution in 1859. It challenged a literal interpretation of the creation story in the Bible and started arguments between scientists and religious leaders, a discussion that still exists today.

One "dream" invention I would like to make a reality is:
_____
_____

Colonization

During this period just about every corner of the world was explored and then claimed by some European country. North and South America were explored first. Then Europeans traveled to and claimed parts of Africa, India, Australia, the Pacific Islands, and the Orient.

All this exploring and colonizing brought a flood of new ideas, new materials, and new information back to Europe. Many Europeans grew rich when the trading business flourished. A new upper class of wealthy manufacturers and merchants developed, replacing the noble class that was destroyed during the revolutions.

This great increase in exploration and colonization was not all positive, though. It often brought such ills as slavery, disease, and oppression to the people in the lands being colonized. Much as in the Middle Ages, the wheat and the weeds of society existed side by side.

An immigrant Church

The Church in the United States is an immigrant Church. The first colonists were mostly Protestants. By the time the colonies broke from England and formed the United States, Protestantism was the unofficial religion of the nation.

In the nineteenth century, large numbers of Catholics began to migrate to America. After suffering from revolutions and wars in Europe, the people saw America as the land of opportunity. So Catholic immigrants, mostly of the uneducated peasant and working classes, fled Europe in large numbers, hoping to find freedom and work in the United States.

They came from Italy, Ireland, Germany, Poland, Belgium, and France. Many, like the Irish and Italians, settled in the large cities on the East Coast and found work in factories and construction. Others went further inland to claim land and begin farming.

But wherever these Catholic immigrants went, the Church—especially the local parish—played a central role in their lives. Those immigrants who did not know English depended on their parish priest to help them get settled and find work. Having little education, they also depended on their parish priest to continue to guide and instruct them.

The first immigrants were eager for their children to get an education. One problem was that most public schools during this time tended to be "anti-Catholic," so the only solution for the Catholic immigrants was to have their children attend a parish school. Almost every Catholic parish provided a Catholic school where the children could learn about their faith along with other subjects.

As a result, ethnic parishes were common. That is, all the Catholic Italians gathered at the "Italian" parish where the sermons were in Italian and the Italian religious customs were practiced. Often the Italian language was taught in the parish school. Similarly, the Irish formed an "Irish" parish and school; the Germans formed a "German" parish and school; and so forth.

Even to this day we sometimes see the effects of these ethnic parishes. For example, in St. Louis there is still an Italian section, an Irish section, a German section, and a Polish section. Gathering around ethnic parishes had positive and negative effects for the community. Positively, it helped people hold on to their faith and their customs and traditions. A negative effect was that it tended to create the idea that Catholics were "foreigners" and a minority in the community. Many parishes were viewed as Catholic "ghettos," creating ethnic prejudices. People believed Catholics, as foreigners, were not loyal to the Constitution, but rather that their loyalty remained with a foreign power—the papacy.

Gradually, the children and grandchildren of these immigrants intermarried with people of other nationalities. Ethnic parishes began to fade.

Today, the Catholic Church in the United States is a vital, educated, generous, and loyal community of the faithful. And it is all due to our great-great-grandparents who often arrived in this country owning nothing but the clothes on their backs and the faith in their hearts.

Currently, a new wave of Catholic immigrants, mostly of Hispanic descent, are settling in the United States. They face many of the same problems of language, poverty, and discrimination as earlier Catholic immigrants from Europe faced. But they enrich our Church in much the same way as our immigrating ancestors did.

The final result—secularism

During the Renaissance, many people believed strongly in the philosophy of humanism, stressing the potential of human accomplishment. Yet no one doubted that God was still the Creator and source of all the beauty and good to be found in the world. Faith still held a respectable place in society.

The focus gradually shifted again during this period of history. All the new discoveries in science and the secularism that followed began to have a negative effect on religion. Science began to replace theology as the most important subject to study. Philosophers and scientists began to teach that reason and science, not faith and religion, were the "salvation" of humanity.

In time, some people began to doubt everything related to faith and religion in general—the existence of God, the existence of an immortal human soul (life after death), the truth of Scripture, the value of prayer. All that began to matter to many people was the material world (secularism).

What's your view?

Secularism exists in our world today. Do you agree or disagree with this statement? Explain your reasoning.

TRIVIA TEASER

The expression *mad as a hatter* originated during this period. People who worked in hat factories often became infected by the chemicals used to treat the beaver skins from which the hats were made. They suffered brain damage and literally went mad.

War, war, war

By now you must have a sense for one fact of history—there have been wars in every age. But this was the period when "modern war" began. In feudal times, most of the fighting took place in a small area. A battle could be won or lost on one field, and a farmer could be plowing in the next.

The introduction of gunpowder changed this situation. Knights and castles were no match for bullets and cannon balls. No matter how skilled the knight was with a horse and sword, a peasant with a musket could now win the battle.

Civilian armies formed, and large-scale wars were fought. No country or person was left untouched. The nineteenth century witnessed many wars fought in Europe, initiated by Napoleon I of France in hopes of expanding his empire, as well as our own Civil War, fought between the North and the South in the 1860s (one of the bloodiest wars ever). In the twentieth century, many powerful nations were drawn into World War I and World War II. The wars not only killed the soldiers, but also bombed and murdered civilians.

Revolution, secularism, colonialism, war—in such a society, the Church definitely had its work cut out for it.

Catechism Connection

The Church and human reason both assert the permanent validity of the *moral law during armed conflict*. "The mere fact that war has regrettably broken out does not mean that everything becomes licit between the warring parties." [*GS* 79§4.] (2312)

THE COMMUNITY'S SPIRITUAL LIFE

The Council of Trent proves effective

The reforms the Council of Trent planned for the Church became a reality during this period. The abuses in the leadership and in monastic life that were common throughout the Middle Ages and into the Renaissance were virtually eliminated. After the council, most popes were worthy, dedicated men. More and more bishops chosen were men of learning and virtue and had a true concern for the people. Priests were well educated in theology and the spiritual life before they were ordained. Those in monasteries and the men and women who joined the newly formed religious communities lived dedicated lives of prayer and service. When an abuse did come to light, the Church quickly corrected the situation.

Given such strong leadership, the laity responded accordingly. They took their faith seriously and acted upon it. Children were commonly instructed in the catechism. Catholic schools were established. Superstitious practices that were common in the Middle Ages disappeared. In their place were regular celebrations of the sacraments and a wide variety of wholesome popular devotions, especially to the Blessed Sacrament and to Mary, the Mother of Jesus.

Good works

One sure sign of the healthy faith of our ancestors during this period was the great increase in service to others. Through the efforts of both religious communities and the laity and the guidance of the Holy Spirit, the good works of the Church were everywhere. Such good works included the establishment of orphanages, hospitals, schools for those who were poor, and homes for society's outcasts.

Many new religious communities were founded out of this dedication to serving in the name of Jesus. Some were small, focusing on a local need and never spreading outside the diocese in which they began. Others grew to become worldwide communities with thousands of members. In any case, many of the faithful in this period received a call to serve others in the name of Jesus—and they responded generously.

List three organizations that you know perform good works in our world today.

Organization:
Good Works:

Organization:
Good Works:

Organization:
Good Works:

 **TRIVIA TEASER**

The University of Notre Dame in South Bend, Indiana, was founded in 1842. It began in a log cabin as a boarding school for boys.

This is one way I provide service to my community:
_____
_____
_____

Will the persecutions ever end?

Yes, there were also persecutions in some countries during this time, the largest taking place during the French Revolution. At one point, the leadership of the French government was taken over by people who hated the Church. They hunted down and imprisoned any priests, religious, and faithful who supported the old government. Many were executed as enemies of the state. Churches and monasteries were seized, altars and sacred objects desecrated, and religious books burned.

At times, missionaries and converts in the Americas, Africa, Asia, and the Pacific Islands were also persecuted and martyred by native peoples who were fearful of or opposed to the gospel.

Another period of persecution occurred during the 1930s and 1940s when Hitler and the Nazis ruled in Germany. Christians and Jews alike were often imprisoned or executed as traitors. The Church's right to teach and preach was revoked. It was much the same in Russia, China, and other countries where communism spread after World War II. As seen throughout history, these persecutions did not eliminate faith, but rather only served to strengthen it.

The Church survived and strengthened throughout this period due to good leadership, a devout laity, dedicated religious, and a commitment to good works. Blessed with these qualities, our ancestors maintained and passed on the faith despite secularism, wars, and the social upheaval that dominated this era. Another quality that helped the Church grow was good teaching, a topic that will be discussed soon.

Scripture Search

Read Mark 10:28–31 and answer the following questions.

1. Have you ever given something up for the sake for the gospel? What did you sacrifice?

   _____
   _____
   _____

2. Of all the things you presently possess, what do you think would be the hardest thing to give up in order to maintain your friendship with Jesus?

   _____
   _____
   _____

THE COMMUNITY'S UNDERSTANDING OF THE GOSPEL MESSAGE

THE COMMUNITY'S MISSION

The challenge of other Christian Churches

When Luther and other religious leaders protested against the Catholic Church in the sixteenth century, they challenged certain abuses and specific beliefs, such as the authority of the pope and the nature of the sacraments. Their goal was to bring about reform—not to destroy Christianity but to strengthen it. They were committed to trying to live according to the basic gospel message. These reformers were dedicated to spreading the gospel and were eventually active in missionary work, just as the Catholic Church was.

This competition put the Catholic Church on the defensive. It was no longer the "only show in town" when it came to Christian faith in the West. The Church could not take it for granted that everyone would believe and accept its teachings. It had to explain and "prove" that its beliefs and teachings were rooted in the teachings of Jesus and the apostles.

So the Church put a great deal of energy into developing its theology and defending ancient teachings. To help the faithful understand these truths, catechisms were developed, containing questions and answers for all the important truths of our faith that were being challenged, such as, "What is a sacrament?" "What is sanctifying grace?" "What is a sacramental?" In the United States, the most famous catechism was the *Baltimore Catechism*, developed in 1885. This catechism was the main text for religion classes in America until 1965.

The challenge of secularism

Protestants were dedicated Christians who shared our basic belief in Jesus. Secular humanists, on the other hand, challenged all religion. They tried to prove that neither God nor Jesus existed. If Jesus did exist, he was just another religious leader like Confucius, Buddha, or Muhammad. Secular humanists challenged the idea that the Bible was God's revelation and questioned the existence of miracles, heaven, hell, and the human soul.

Secular humanists taught that science and reason, not the cross and faith, were where "salvation" could be found. They claimed that Church leaders held people in ignorance just to control them and get their money. Secularists attacked the Church through their teaching at universities and by writing popular books and newspapers.

In some cases, a government was controlled by secularists. When that happened, the government passed laws to make it difficult for the Church to teach, sometimes by closing Catholic schools and universities. The government imposed high taxes on Church property and banned certain religious communities from the country.

This intellectual and political persecution started slowly. But as the spirit of science and secularism grew, the Church found itself under very serious attack.

From the home office in Rome

If someone who believed in secularism asked you why you remain a strong disciple of Jesus, what reasons would you give? In a small group, compile a "top ten" list of reasons as to why your faith in Jesus comes first.

Top ten reasons why faith in Jesus comes first

1.
2.
3.
4.
5.
6.
7.
8.
9.
10.

The Church's counterattack

The Church now saw itself at war, fighting for its survival in this new age of secularism. One response was the First Vatican Council, held in Rome from 1869 to 1870. The council defined papal infallibility, noting the pope and the bishops in union with him are the Church's supreme authority in doctrine and morality. It declared that the pope and the bishops in union with him cannot err under certain conditions when officially explaining the gospel and God's revelation. The council also condemned a number of popular errors the secularists were teaching. As we'll see, this council had both a "good news" and "bad news" effect. In the end, the Church succeeded in reasserting its authority to speak in the name of Jesus and demonstrating that Christianity (and the Church) was not "dead" as many secularists claimed.

There's no doubt that the Church lost a great deal of influence during this era. In the Middle Ages, virtually everyone in Europe was Catholic and the Church influenced all of society. By 1950, less than half of Europe practiced any faith at all. Contrary to all predictions, the Church was able to survive the serious threat of secularism. What was lost in terms of numbers of believers, the Church gained in terms of the depth and understanding of the faith among those who still believed.

What is one area of your faith life that you feel is "dead"? How can you bring it back to life?

_____
_____
_____
_____
_____

TRIVIA TEASER

In 1891, Pope Leo XIII wrote the famous encyclical letter *Rerum Novarum*. In it, he defended the rights of the working class. An encyclical letter is a letter written by a pope to instruct the entire Church and is considered a form of official teaching.

Mission work

Note that the sections "The Community's Understanding of the Gospel Message" and "The Community's Mission" are combined in this chapter. These two activities are so closely connected during this period that they can't really be separated.

Although the Church was losing membership in Europe, it was gaining new converts throughout the rest of the world. In all the distant corners of the earth, people who had never even heard of Jesus came to believe. Brave and faith-filled missionaries brought the gospel to people in India, China, Japan, the Pacific Islands, Indochina, and Africa. In their work they also established churches, schools, and hospitals.

Many missionary efforts took place right in Europe and in other Catholic countries. The Church made efforts to call back to faith many people who had left the Church because of secularism. All Catholics were called upon to give good example and to defend their faith against the errors of secularism.

In their travels, the missionaries had wonderful adventures yet endured all kinds of hardships. Sometimes they were martyred for their efforts. But because of their work, the Church grew in all these lands.

The work of our ancestors (some were possibly your great-great-grandparents) must have been successful. Today over one-fourth of all people on earth consider themselves members of the Catholic Church. Our Church remains the largest single faith on earth.

THE COMMUNITY'S ORGANIZATION

Unity and uniformity

Faced with the challenge of Protestantism and then secularism, Church leaders had very important roles to play in defending the faith during these years. They did this in several ways. First, the pope and his assistants in Rome took on a much greater leadership role. They kept closer tabs on the bishops and the priests throughout the world. Bishops were appointed because of their loyalty and their sound theology. They were also directed to report regularly to the pope. All priests were required to study the same basic theology in the seminaries where they trained.

In turn the bishops played a similar role in their own dioceses. They checked in on the priests and what was happening in the parishes. Rules for celebrating the sacraments were strictly enforced. Catholic schools and universities were required to teach certain programs.

As a result, by the end of the nineteenth century, Catholics could go almost anywhere in the world—except for the Eastern Rites—and find the Mass and other sacraments all celebrated exactly the same way. All the faithful were taught the same truths and explanations. Unity and uniformity were key ideas in the Church. Loyalty to the pope, to the local bishop, and to the parish priest were all considered signs of being a good Catholic. This kind of unity, loyalty, and uniformity among Catholics is one of the reasons why the Church not only survived the challenges of this era, but actually grew stronger in the process.

TRIVIA TEASER

Pope Saint Pius X restored the practice of allowing children to receive Holy Communion at age seven. Before that it had become a custom to wait until age twelve or older before receiving the sacrament

Scripture Search

Read John 17:20–26. What prayers does Jesus have for all believers as they strive toward unity?

- That they may _____

- That they may _____

- That they may _____

Monarchy, democracy, and the Church

One difficulty the Church faced during this time was that the popes and bishops were regarded in much the same way as the kings and nobles were during the Middle Ages. Sometimes they even acted in a similar manner.

After the reforms of the Council of Trent, popes and bishops did not try to live or act like kings and nobles anymore. Yet to the people, they still appeared like the rulers of feudalism because of their titles, royal robes, crowns, and thrones. In addition, the pope and the college of bishops did have supreme authority in the Church, a system that closely resembled a monarchy with one ruler. So along with opposing the kings and nobility of this time, many revolutionaries also saw the Church as an enemy.

Many people thus began to believe that the Church and its leaders opposed democracy. The secularists were quick to promote this view. The First Vatican Council, which defined papal infallibility and condemned many modern errors, was interpreted by people to mean that the Church needed only one ruler (the pope) and was not in favor of scientific progress. The people made a terrible misinterpretation when they believed these statements.

"I therefore, the prisoner in the Lord, beg you to lead a life worthy of the calling to which you have been called, with all humility and gentleness, with patience, bearing with one another in love, making every effort to maintain the unity of the Spirit in the bond of peace. There is one body and one Spirit, just as you were called to the one hope of your calling, one Lord, one faith, one baptism, one God and Father of all, who is above all and through all and in all" (Ephesians 4:1–6).

Briefly discuss ways that people your age can bring unity to your local parish and community.

Here is one way I can bring unity to my family this week:
_____
_____

Pause to Pray

Reader #1: Jesus, help us remember to pray for the leaders of our Church and our country. We pray . . .

All: Lord, hear our prayer.

Reader #2: Jesus, help us always remain united with you and your Church. We pray . . .

All: Lord, hear our prayer.

Reader #3: Jesus, help us reach out to those who do not feel united with your Church. We pray . . .

All: Lord, hear our prayer.

HOMEWORK

Knowing that it is easy to get caught up in the materialism of our world (secularism), evaluate your own possessions and decide which five things you would keep if all else had to be given away. Then after each item, explain its importance and value to you.

1.

Value:

2.

Value:

3.

Value:

4.

Value:

5.

Value:

UP TO THE MINUTE— 1950 C.E.–PRESENT

Growing up

Our lives are built upon change. Take a survey of your own life and notice how much you have changed since childhood. List five examples that show how you are different now than when you were younger.

At age _____ I used to _____

Now I _____

At age _____ I used to _____

Now I _____

At age _____ I used to _____

Now I _____

At age _____ I used to _____

Now I _____

At age _____ I used to _____

Now I _____

1959–75 C.E. The Vietnam War

1962–65 C.E. The Second Vatican Council held in Rome

1962 C.E. The rock group The Rolling Stones formed

1963 C.E. President John F. Kennedy was assassinated in Dallas, Texas

1968 C.E. Martin Luther King Jr. was assassinated in Memphis, Tennessee

1969 C.E. Neil Armstrong and Edwin Aldrin, part of the Apollo 11 mission, became the first humans to walk on the moon

Welcome to the present

This age is a time of rapid change. As society has progressed, these years are known by many different names, including the Age of Post-Industrial Society, the Nuclear Age, the Communication Age, the Computer Age, and the Electronic Era. We've experienced an explosion of new knowledge, new inventions, and new discoveries that matches those of the Renaissance in the sixteenth century. Much of it is amazing—moon walks, space shuttles, satellite communication, computers, and heart transplants.

As before, these changes are a combination of both advancements and downfalls. With television and satellites, we now watch what's happening on the other side of the world—while it's happening! Unfortunately, what we often see isn't very pleasant—wars, famine, poverty, terrorism. Our large world is a "small world" now, yet it's more divided than ever. We are sacrificing the earth for development by destroying our natural resources and the environment. Not only that, technology has provided us with enough nuclear weapons to destroy the world several times.

Yet in this modern era, the gospel message remains the same as when it was first proclaimed—the reign of God is among us, trust in God's love and in turn, love one another. But when Jesus first proclaimed his message in the first century, people believed the earth was flat and the stars were gods. The challenge for the Church today is to translate Jesus' simple message into a language and a lifestyle that makes sense in a time when people can shop for groceries with a modem and a computer. The Church's effort to renew or update the gospel message is the focus of this final chapter.

The approach for this chapter is a little different, though. Rather than using the usual five-part division, this chapter centers on two aspects of our Church—how the Second Vatican Council has affected the Church and the faith life of the community.

TRIVIA TEASER

Since Vatican Council II, the single most popular topic of study by adult Catholics has been Scripture.

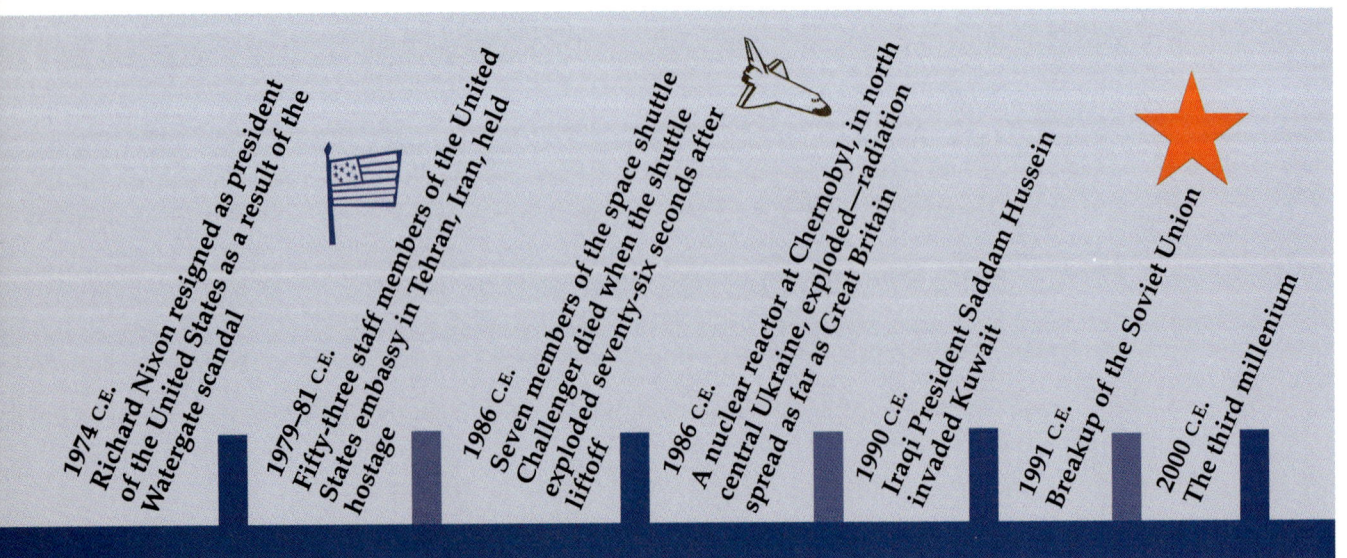

1974 C.E. Richard Nixon resigned as president of the United States as a result of the Watergate scandal

1979–81 C.E. Fifty-three staff members of the United States embassy in Tehran, Iran, held hostage

1986 C.E. Seven members of the space shuttle Challenger died when the shuttle exploded seventy-six seconds after liftoff

1986 C.E. A nuclear reactor at Chernobyl, in north central Ukraine, exploded—radiation spread as far as Great Britain

1990 C.E. Iraqi President Saddam Hussein invaded Kuwait

1991 C.E. Breakup of the Soviet Union

2000 C.E. The third millenium

VATICAN COUNCIL II (1962–65)

A different kind of council

Most of the great councils in the Church, beginning with the first meeting in Jerusalem in 49 C.E., were called to settle a major problem or error in the Church. A good example would be how the Council of Trent dealt with the issue of Protestantism.

But the Second Vatican Council was different. Its main purpose wasn't to fight against an error or heresy. Instead, Pope John XXIII called the bishops of the world into a council because the Church needed to renew itself with the guidance of the Holy Spirit. The goal of the council was to bring about a renewal in our understanding of the faith and to breathe new energy and excitement into our lives as disciples of Jesus.

Since the Council of Trent four hundred years earlier, the world had acquired new knowledge in the areas of science, the development of the Bible, the work of the apostles, and the early Church. The language used to explain Church beliefs in the 1500s was difficult to understand in the 1960s. In order for truths about sin, grace, salvation, and sacrament to be clearly understood by people in the modern age, the truths needed to be put into modern language.

So when the bishops and others gathered for the Second Vatican Council, one of the main tasks Pope John XXIII assigned the council was to integrate Church teaching with this new knowledge and new ways of speaking.

TRIVIA TEASER

Pope John XXIII, who called the Second Vatican Council in January 1959 at the age of 78, died after the first session of the council. His successor, Pope Paul VI, presided over the concluding three sessions.

Going backwards to move forward

In order to bring the Church into the modern age, the Second Vatican Council had to look to the past—at the way the apostles and first disciples lived, what they believed, and what they taught.

Over the nineteen centuries since Jesus and the apostles lived, society influenced the Church in each period. The result was like a snowball rolling down from the top of a mountain. As the small snowball rolls down, it picks up new layers of snow. And with the snow, rocks, sticks, and clutter get mixed in.

The teachings and practices of the Church were a lot like that snowball. Over the centuries, the core message of Jesus and the faith life of the early disciples got covered with extra layers of laws, customs, and practices. Some practices made sense at the time, but sometimes no longer made sense in the modern age. People could no longer see the inner core of the snowball and often believed the outer layers to be the truth they were to follow.

So the council members studied history— just as you are doing. They peeled off the layers to arrive at the core of the Church. Their research included checking out what the apostles and the early Church did, when certain practices started, why they were started, and if they still had value today. Those that still had value, the council kept. The practices that were no longer essential or valuable to the faith were dropped by the council.

In many instances, the council restored practices of the early Church. In fact, some of the greatest changes Vatican II introduced weren't changes at all. They brought the faithful back to the core ideas and ideals of the apostles that had been learned from Jesus.

The twentieth century

Before the Second Vatican Council, the Mass was celebrated differently than it is today. For each of the following pre-Vatican II practices, write how it has changed in the twentieth century.

- All Masses (except in the Eastern Rites) said in Latin.

- Only the priest touched the host with his hands.

- People sat in silence and watched.

- Only altar servers said the Latin responses.

- The priest faced an altar built against the wall of the sanctuary.

- Everyone fasted from midnight until Mass before receiving Communion.

What's your view?

Make one prediction that you believe could occur within the next century for each of the following aspects of the Church.

1. The Church's relationship with society
   _____
   _____

2. The Church's community life and spirituality
   _____
   _____

3. How the gospel is taught
   _____
   _____

4. The Church's mission
   _____
   _____

5. The Church's structure and organization
   _____
   _____

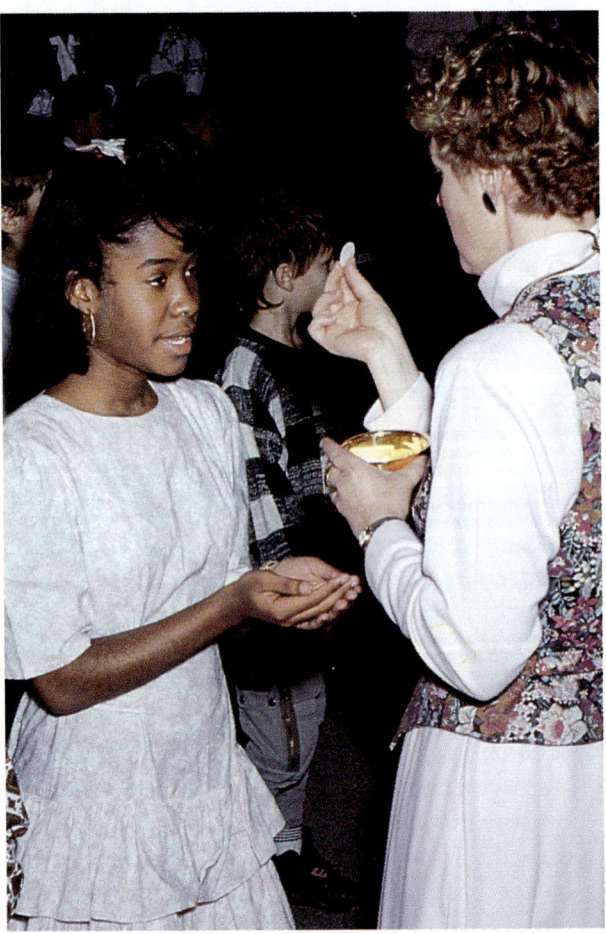

WHEN I WAS YOUNGER...

Interview someone, such as a grandparent, who was living during the time of the Second Vatican Council. Write a paragraph about what you learn. Be sure to ask how the person felt at the time about the changes the Church was experiencing.

I interviewed _____

What I learned:

_____
_____
_____
_____
_____
_____
_____
_____

Reaction to renewal

For most adults in 1960, the only Church they knew was the Church based on the teachings of the Council of Trent, held four hundred years earlier. People believed that the practices and teachings of the Church were exactly what Jesus and the apostles taught. Therefore it was wrong to make any changes.

Along came Vatican II and renewal in the Church. It's understandable that many people were confused, angered, and frightened by the teachings and the "new" practices introduced by the council.

Nevertheless, the Church succeeded in bringing about renewal and updating its understanding of the unchanging truths of our faith. Yet the work begun by the Second Vatican Council is far from over. Many people still don't fully understand or appreciate what the council tried to do. Even today there are some people who would like the Church to return to the teachings and practices of the Council of Trent.

As a young disciple, this is one of your challenges as a Christian—to complete the renewal in the Church begun by Vatican II.

Dialogue Corner

Each period in history is usually given a name that sums up an important or common quality of that time. For example, the world has experienced such eras as the Age of Enlightenment and the Renaissance.

Thinking about our Church today, what would be a good name for the present? What will this time in history be referred to in textbooks in the future? In a group of four, discuss the events of our time and write down a term for this period in history. Be prepared to explain your reasoning for choosing this title.

_____

Compare your title with that of other groups. As a class, come to an agreement on the most appropriate name for the present time.

FAITH LIFE OF THE COMMUNITY

The final results

The changes brought about in the life of the community by the Second Vatican Council fall into four general areas: (1) Scripture, (2) sacraments and liturgy, (3) leadership and responsibility, and (4) ecumenism. We will examine each of these areas in this section.

Scripture

From the fourth century until the twentieth century, little changed in how people read and understood the Bible. They knew it was God's word, God's special revelation to us. But in actuality, most people did not fully understand the Bible, such as how it came to be written down, the exact meaning of some words, or the intention the authors first had in writing a particular passage.

Recently, teachings have begun to help us read the Bible with "new eyes." The original meanings of words and the intention of the writers have become more clear to us. The Bible is even more a "living word." By reading and studying the Scriptures, we are able to discover new meanings and to gain deeper knowledge about God, the Church, and ourselves.

> *"Come to me, all you that are weary and are carrying heavy burdens, and I will give you rest. Take my yoke upon you, and learn from me; for I am gentle and humble in heart, and you will find rest for your souls. For my yoke is easy, and my burden is light."*
>
> —Matthew 11:28–30

How can you apply these words of Jesus to your own life? Give an example of a specific time when these words will be of help to you.

_____
_____
_____

Sacraments and liturgy

Perhaps one of the biggest changes since Vatican II is the way we understand and celebrate the sacraments and the Mass. The renewal of the Mass went much farther than simply translating the Latin into the language of the people. Each of the seven sacraments was studied, and the meaning and purpose of each one was explained in detail. Finally, the rites used to celebrate the sacraments were renewed to fit their original meaning and purpose and today's needs.

Because the sacraments are at the very heart of our Church, Vatican II knew that to truly renew the Church, we must renew our sacramental life. This renewal was one of the greatest achievements of the Second Vatican Council.

Describe one time in your life when you have seen or personally experienced one of the sacraments being celebrated. What impact did it make on your life?

_____
_____
_____
_____

Leadership and responsibility

Ever since Constantine's decree that granted religious freedom in 313 C.E., a gap gradually began to develop between the clergy and the people. This division grew wider as monasteries and religious communities developed. In time, most people thought that the clergy and the religious (monks, nuns, brothers, sisters) were the only ones responsible for the life and work of the Church. They came to believe that the "people in the pew" had no special role or responsibility in promoting the message of Jesus.

Vatican II renewed the understanding that spreading the gospel message is the responsibility of all who are baptized in the Church. The council stressed that the clergy and the laity (the "people in the pew") are partners in carrying out the mission of the Church. The responsibility for Church leadership, while resting in a special way upon the pope and the bishops, is also a duty to be shared by all.

This concept of shared responsibility has led to many changes in the overall organization and work of the Church. Lay people now serve as lectors and Eucharistic ministers at Mass; they also play key roles in helping the pastor direct the parish. They participate in teaching, working with those who are sick, and preparing couples for marriage.

The laity now share in many of the ministries and leadership positions of the Church that once belonged only to the clergy and the religious. In many ways this renewal of the role of the laity is a return to how it was back in the time of the apostles and the early Church.

 **Catechism Connection**

Lay people who possess the required qualities can be admitted permanently to the ministries of lector and acolyte. [Cf. CIC, can. 230§1.] When the necessity of the Church warrants it and when ministers are lacking, lay persons, even if they are not lectors or acolytes, can also supply for certain of their offices, namely, to exercise the ministry of the word, to preside over liturgical prayers, to confer Baptism, and to distribute Holy Communion in accord with the prescriptions of law. [CIC, can. 230§3.] (903)

 **TRIVIA TEASER**

The United States bishops in two pastoral letters—*The Challenge of Peace: God's Promise and Our Response* (1983) and *Economic Justice for All* (1986)—called the faithful to work for a more peaceful and just society. These documents are unique in that the bishops asked for input from the faithful as the letters were developed.

An active role in the Church

List the ministries lay people perform in your parish.

Choose two ministries that you would like to participate in and explain why.

1.

2.

Have you met... *Dorothy Day (1897–1980)*

Dorothy Day was a convert to the Catholic faith in 1929. As an active lay person in the Church, Dorothy felt a strong Christian commitment to aiding those who lived in poverty in New York City. Through her ministry, she founded the Catholic Worker Movement and established Catholic Worker Houses, which provided food, shelter, clothing, and dignity for those in need. She has been proposed for sainthood.

I wanted life, and I wanted the abundant life. I wanted it for others too. I did not want just the few, the missionary-minded people like the Salvation Army, to be kind to the poor.... I wanted everyone to be kind.

—Dorothy Day

Some people think the present shortage in vocations to the priesthood and religious life, though unfortunate, has a good side effect. It is helping all the faithful realize that they share the responsibility to carry out the work of the Church.

The religious community founded by Mother Teresa to work with the poorest of the poor is the fastest growing religious community in the world today.

Ecumenism between Catholics and Protestants

From the time of Luther onward, Catholics viewed Protestants as enemies. Protestants felt the same way toward Catholics. Since the Council of Trent in the sixteenth century, the Church spent a lot of its energy protecting the faith—and the faithful—from Protestant teaching and influence.

The Second Vatican Council called a halt to this defensive approach. It summoned the Church to begin to focus on what we have in common with other Christian religions rather than continuing to focus on our differences.

As a result there has been a general movement to cooperate and share with our Protestant brothers and sisters in common efforts to promote gospel values. In preparation for the millennium jubilee, the Catholic Church initiated further efforts to understand and to overcome our differences in belief.

It isn't easy to overcome four hundred years of bitterness. And there remain some very serious differences in our beliefs. But at least we are beginning to work together in many important ways, with a strong hope that someday "all may be one" again, as Jesus wants us to be.

TRIVIA TEASER

Though there are still serious doctrinal differences, the relationship between the Catholic and Protestant Churches is the best it has been since the time of Martin Luther. Much of this is due to the work and the spirit of cooperation developed by Vatican II.

The changing relationship between Church and state

Throughout history, the Church and the state have shared many different relationships. When the apostles began to proclaim the gospel in the Roman Empire after Pentecost, the Church was considered an enemy of the state. It was met with hostility and persecution—much like what Jesus had experienced. But the Church grew despite this hostility. Persecution only served to strengthen the faith of our ancestors.

In time, with the help of Constantine's Edict of Milan in 313 C.E., the Church gradually became partners with the state. This partnership worked for a period of time because the state was in decline and needed the help of the Church to maintain order and to govern the people. But as the state grew weaker, the Church grew stronger. It grew so strong, in fact, that the Church was virtually identical with the state for many years during the Middle Ages. The popes and other Church leaders were also society's leaders. The ideals of the gospel influenced every aspect of society. This worked for a while, but eventually the effects from the partnership actually weakened the Church. Church leaders were often more involved in politics than in proclaiming and teaching the gospel. So the kings and princes, jealous of the power the popes and bishops held, began to compete with the Church for control of the people.

After the Middle Ages and the Protestant Revolt, the great nations of Europe developed. The secular rulers regained control of society. So the Church and the state worked out a compromise, agreeing that the Church would focus primarily on the spiritual life of the people. The state would handle the government, taxes, and public policies.

There was a problem with this arrangement, though. People began to separate their faith life from their everyday life in society. Sometimes faith and religion became practices for Sundays only. Religion didn't have anything to do with how you lived and worked the rest of the week.

So when the Second Vatican Council asked how the Church should relate to the state and to society, it had a lot of history to draw upon. Being totally separated from society and focusing only on the spiritual had not worked. We are called to live the gospel every day, not simply think about it on Sundays alone. We are to act as Jesus did, with concern for the poor, for injustice, for violence, and for the strong overpowering the weak.

But having the Church control the state wasn't the answer either, as was learned from the Middle Ages. So since Vatican II, the Church's role in society has been more of a prophetic influence, calling the people to justice and peace through its teachings and its example.

In a historic visit to the United Nations, Pope Paul VI called all world leaders to strive for peace. Although there weren't any instant miracles, this calling emphasized to the world that the Church was dedicated to helping nations work out differences in peaceful ways. Several pastoral letters have called all countries to work toward an end to nuclear weapons and for all people to work together to help the poor throughout the world.

So the Church today is clearly committed to shaping the everyday life of society according to gospel ideals. It is concerned about nuclear weapons, abortion, hunger, those suffering from AIDS, political oppression—all the evils that afflict people in society today. But in doing so, the Church no longer seeks the political control it possessed during the Middle Ages. Like Jesus, today's Church is clearly a part of the greater world—not to control it by force and power, but to redeem it through love. You are being called to share in this—the mission of our Church.

SIGN OF THE TIMES

Choose one of the following road signs or use one of your own and write about how you think the sign symbolizes the Church today.
- Stop
- Yield
- Caution: Falling Rocks
- No Passing Zone
- Road Construction Ahead
- End Construction
- Caution: Workers Ahead

A continuing story

The history of the Church is a story of wheat and weeds growing side by side. Although we may study its history, the story of our Church is never-ending, continuing to develop every day. You are an active part of this continuing story.

The events of history continue to have an effect on the community today. This is evident in how the Second Vatican Council continues to shape you as a disciple of Jesus. The effects of the council on the Church and the community are very much present today.

As we discussed earlier, all the events in our history as a community of disciples form the patches of a quilt. The common thread that ties all these patches together is the faith and friendship of Jesus the community shares.

One purpose of studying the history of the Church is so that we can learn from past events and grow as a community of believers. Our task now is to learn from the stories of our ancestors and to model their positive examples as work for our Church today.

This is your challenge. Are you ready to be a part of the story?

Reflection

"I do not call you servants any longer, because the servant does not know what the master is doing; but I have called you friends, because I have made known to you everything that I have heard from my Father. You did not choose me but I chose you. And I appointed you to go and bear fruit, fruit that will last, so that the Father will give you whatever you ask him in my name. I am giving you these commands so that you may love one another" (John 15:15–17).

Briefly discuss ways in which we can carry on the example of our ancestors in faith.

Of the ancestors in faith that you have learned about, who do you most want to follow? Why?
___
___
___

Pause to Pray

Reader #1: There is a wonderful old story
Written in a time long gone:
It is the gospel according to
Matthew, Mark, Luke, and John.

Reader #2: The Gospels were given to show us
The power of God's love divine;
May that story be told again
In the writing of your life and mine.

Reader #3: People read and admire the gospel
With its love so inspiring and true,
But what do they say and think of
The gospel according to you?

Reader #4: You are writing a gospel,
A chapter every day,
By deeds that you do,
By the words that you say.

Reader #5: You are writing each day a gospel,
Take care that the writing is true.
For the only gospel some will read—
Is the gospel according to you.

All: Jesus, help us bear the kind of fruit that endures.
Help us do our part in spreading your gospel message.
Help us follow your command to love others. Amen.

HOMEWORK

Summing it up

Now that you've finished the course, jot down your responses to each of the following questions.

1. What do you think was the most **important** thing you learned about the Church in this course? Explain your reasoning.
   _____
   _____
   _____

2. What was the most **surprising** thing you learned about the Church? Why was it surprising?
   _____
   _____
   _____

3. Explain the most **interesting** topic you learned with regard to the Church.
   _____
   _____
   _____

4. What was the most **helpful** thing you learned? Why?
   _____
   _____
   _____

5. What era did you find the most interesting? The least interesting? Explain why you choose these periods of history.
   _____
   _____
   _____

6. List three things you'd like to learn more about regarding the Church.
   _____
   _____
   _____

APPENDIX I: SAINTS FOR OUR TIME

Saint Barnabas (June 11)

Saint Barnabas was a companion of Paul on his first missionary journey to the Gentiles. After setting up the Christian community on Cyprus, Barnabas was martyred for the faith.

Saint Charles Borromeo (November 4)

The Church did not ignore the concerns of Protestant reformers. Leaders like Charles Borromeo, an Italian cardinal, worked hard to correct the abuses that had contributed to divisions in Christianity. Because of his efforts to reform the training of priests, Saint Charles Borromeo is the patron saint of seminarians.

Saint Catherine of Siena (April 29)

As a teenager, Saint Catherine joined the Dominicans as a lay member. She volunteered in hospitals, caring for people with leprosy, cancer, and bubonic plague. At one time, the pope was living in France, and she wrote to him, urging him to return to Rome. She brought members of two quarreling groups within the Church together to try to settle their differences. Catherine worked hard to bring peace to the Church.

Saint Cyril of Jerusalem (March 18)

Saint Cyril was a great teacher of the early Church who diligently studied the Scriptures. He was put in charge of instructing catechumens. Saint Cyril designed a program of group instruction due to the lack of teachers for one-on-one instruction. His *Catecheses* provides us with valuable insight into the instruction given to catechumens of the fourth century.

Saint John Baptist de la Salle (April 7)

John came from a wealthy French family, but he gave his life and his wealth to educating poor children. He founded the Brothers of the Christian Schools (the Christian Brothers) to open educational opportunities to all people. Saint John Baptist de la Salle is the patron saint of teachers.

Blessed Katherine Drexel (March 3)

Blessed Katherine was a wealthy Philadelphia-born woman who spent her fortune on others, founding schools for Native Americans and African Americans. She reached out to many forgotten peoples and made them feel welcome in the Church. Katherine was the founder of the Sisters of the Blessed Sacrament on behalf of Indians and Colored People (as they were known then). She was beatified by Pope John Paul II in 1988.

Saint Rose Philippine Duchesne (November 18)

Rose was forced out of her convent for ten years as a result of the French Revolution. Her baptismal call took her from revolutionary France to the United States frontier. As a Sister of the Sacred Heart, she built log-cabin schools, fought forest fires, and shared the good news with people of all races and cultures. She was called the *woman who prays always*.

Saint Ignatius of Loyola (July 31)

Ignatius was born into a noble family in northern Spain. He was educated in the royal court and became a soldier. While recuperating from a battle wound, Ignatius read a book about the saints that changed his life. Once recovered, Ignatius spent much time praying, reflecting on his life, and making pilgrimages. While studying theology, he gathered together a group of men. They took vows of poverty, chastity, and obedience and were ordained in 1537. Later Ignatius drew up a rule of life for the group, now known as the *Society of Jesus*, or the Jesuits.

Saint Jerome (September 30)

Saint Jerome devoted much of his life to study of the Bible. He translated the books of the Old Testament directly from the original Hebrew into Latin, a language the people of his time could understand. He opened the family story of faith to all Christians. Jerome's Latin translation, called the *Vulgate*, became the standard translation for the Catholic Church for centuries.

Pope John XXIII

This twentieth-century pope has not been officially canonized. He was loved by people all over the world for the way in which he led and served the Church. Pope John XXIII gathered the world's bishops for the Second Vatican Council. This great meeting helped the Church bring Jesus' good news to the modern world.

Saint Charles Lwanga and Companions (June 3)

Saint Charles was a young servant of the king of Uganda. When the king commanded his servants to join in the immoral activities of his court, Charles and twenty-one other young Christians refused. They were killed for following their consciences.

Venerable Catherine McAuley

Catherine, born in Dublin, Ireland, recognized the plight of those who were poor and opened a House of Mercy to serve their needs. In 1831, with the help of the local archbishop, Catherine founded a community of women to serve those in need. Some members of the community came to the United States to carry on this work, which continues to this day. They are known as the Religious Sisters of Mercy.

Saint Thomas More (June 22)

Saint Thomas More was a married lawyer who became Chancellor of England under Henry VIII. Later when the king wanted to divorce Catherine of Aragon and marry Anne Boleyn, Thomas sided with the Church. He was beheaded for his refusal to sign the Act of Supremacy, which recognized the king as head of the Church in England.

Saint John Neumann (January 5)

John Neumann came to the United States as a missionary from what is now the Czech Republic. He served European immigrants on the American frontier, traveling on horseback. The loneliness of missionary life drew him to join the Redemptorist Order. Later, John was named bishop of Philadelphia.

Blessed Frederic Ozanam (September 9)

When Frederic was a young man, his friends challenged him to live out his beliefs in his everyday life. Frederic founded the Society of Saint Vincent de Paul. Today the Society of Saint Vincent de Paul has members in more than 120 countries.

Saints Perpetua and Felicity (March 7)

Perpetua and Felicity were young mothers in the North African city of Carthage. They were imprisoned, tortured, and killed for their faith in God.

Saint Polycarp (February 23)

Saint Polycarp was appointed bishop of Smyrna by John, the apostle. Because Christians were a minority in Smyrna, he faced many difficulties there. At the age of 86, he was arrested by Roman soldiers who demanded that he renounce Christ, and when he refused, he was burned at the stake.

Saint Martin de Porres (November 3)

Saint Martin was born in Peru, the son of a Spanish noble and a free black woman. Because of his mixed background, he suffered great injustices. Martin learned about medicine and helped poor people who were sick. As a Dominican lay brother, he founded numerous hospitals throughout Peru and continued to serve and care for people from all walks of life. Saint Martin is the patron saint of interracial justice.

Archbishop Arnulfo Romero

Archbishop Romero was an El Salvadoran priest, who became bishop of Santiago de Maria in 1974, and was installed as archbishop of San Salvador in 1977. Every week during the celebration of the Eucharist, Romero read the names of people who had been mistreated or killed by those in power. He wanted justice for all people, not just the rich. Romero was shot by an assassin on March 24, 1980, while he was celebrating Mass.

Saul (Saint Paul) (January 29)

Saul was a devoted Pharisee who persecuted Christians because he believed they were destroying the Jewish religion. When Saul experienced the risen Jesus himself, on the road to Damascus, he turned his life around completely and became a Christian. Paul believed that Jesus was the Messiah sent by God to save all people from the power of sin and eternal death. This was the message he preached as a missionary leader in the early Church. He wrote many letters that have become part of the New Testament and are read at the celebration of the sacraments. Paul was executed in Rome for his faith in Jesus. The Church celebrates Paul's conversion on January 29.

Saint Elizabeth Ann Seton (January 4)

Elizabeth Seton, a widow with five children, found comfort in the Catholic Church and in turn gave the Church her great energy and strength. She became a teacher and founded the Sisters of Charity to teach Catholics who were poor.

Saint Edith Stein (August 9)

Edith Stein was a Jewish philosopher and teacher. She became a Catholic and entered a Carmelite convent. Her writings testify to the presence of God's saving love in the Jewish and Christian traditions. When the Nazis occupied the Netherlands during World War II, they began persecuting the Jews there. Because she was of Jewish origin, Stein was arrested and sent to a death camp at Auschwitz, where she was executed.

Saint Teresa of Avila (October 15)

Teresa was born in Spain into a large, noble family of Jewish ancestry. After being a nun in a Carmelite monastery for twenty years, she underwent conversion and dedicated herself to reforming the Carmelite order. She wrote about prayer and spiritual wisdom and was named one of the first women doctors of the Church.

Saint Thérèse of Lisieux (October 1)

Thérèse, a Carmelite nun, entered the convent at the age of 15. She believed that love "is the vocation that includes all others." Thérèse spent nine and a half years in the convent before her death from tuberculosis at the age of 24. She wrote that even the simplest actions are holy if done with great love.

APPENDIX II: YOUR CATHOLIC HERITAGE

What Catholics Believe

Apostles' Creed

I [We] believe in God, the Father almighty,
   creator of heaven and earth.

I [We] believe in Jesus Christ, his only Son, our Lord.
   He was conceived by the power of the Holy Spirit
   and born of the Virgin Mary.
   He suffered under Pontius Pilate,
   was crucified, died, and was buried.
   He descended to the dead.
   On the third day he rose again.
   He ascended into heaven,
   and is seated at the right hand of the Father.
   He will come again to judge the living and the dead.

I [We] believe in the Holy Spirit,
   the holy catholic Church,
   the communion of saints,
   the forgiveness of sins,
   the resurrection of the body,
   and the life everlasting. Amen.

Nicene Creed

We believe in one God, the Father, the Almighty, maker of heaven and earth, of all that is seen and unseen.

We believe in one Lord, Jesus Christ, the only Son of God, eternally begotten of the Father, God from God, Light from Light, true God from true God, begotten, not made, one in Being with the Father. Through him all things were made. For us men and for our salvation he came down from heaven: by the power of the Holy Spirit he was born of the Virgin Mary, and became man. For our sake he was crucified under Pontius Pilate; he suffered, died, and was buried. On the third day he rose again in fulfillment of the Scriptures; he ascended into heaven and is seated at the right hand of the Father. He will come again in glory to judge the living and the dead, and his kingdom will have no end.

We believe in the Holy Spirit, the Lord, the giver of life, who proceeds from the Father and the Son. With the Father and the Son he is worshiped and glorified. He has spoken through the Prophets. We believe in one, holy, catholic, and apostolic Church. We acknowledge one baptism for the forgiveness of sins. We look for the resurrection of the dead, and the life of the world to come. Amen.